THE TREASURE UPSTAIRS

By the same author in Pan Books

BELOW STAIRS

CLIMBING THE STAIRS

THE MARGARET POWELL COOKERY BOOK

The Treasure Upstairs

MARGARET POWELL

UNABRIDGED

PAN BOOKS LTD : LONDON

First published 1970 by Peter Davies.
This edition published 1972 by Pan Books Ltd,
33 Tothill Street, London, SW1.

ISBN 0 330 23392 0

*Printed in Great Britain
by Richard Clay (The Chaucer Press), Ltd,
Bungay, Suffolk*

INTRODUCTION

SINCE this book is called *The Treasure Upstairs*, I must begin by defining a 'treasure'. She – because all treasures are shes – is one of a fast-vanishing race. One not only valuable in herself but valuable because of her rarity. She is the jewel of the family crown, the open sesame of connubial bliss. She is the 'Domestic Treasure'. Employers dream of acquiring one. Her value is above rubies, yet her price is small. A treasure is an inexhaustible well of hard work, gives loyal and willing service, and never minds being put upon. She is friendly without being familiar, cheerful yet sympathetic, and never mutters when she's asked to act beyond the call of duty. She must, of course, be willing to shop and baby-sit, and is relied upon to provide a fund of amusing anecdotes which her employers can relate at dinner parties, thus ensuring that they keep way ahead of the Joneses. She must be jealously guarded by her employers and any of their friends making overtures to her must immediately be ostracized. Friends are easier to come by than treasures.

There are two types still extant. There's the one who has been in the same family all her working life, who started as one of a large staff and stayed on through all their adversities until now she alone is left. I received a letter from such a one recently. She told me how her Madam had become poorer, older and frailer until at last she needed constant attention and how, rather than let her go into a home, she had studied nursing so that she could look after her. This she had done for the same money that she'd been getting for the last twenty years. A pittance. Now that's a treasure. Someone who would devote their whole life to service. Some people have accused me of knocking this kind of person. I haven't. What I have knocked is the employer who expected that kind of behaviour without giving anything in return. Obviously her Madam had, because nobody can give in this way without getting some deep appreciation back for it.

Mind you, I would never have done it even if I'd ever worked for anyone like she did, but it doesn't stop me from admiring her; even from wishing I could be the same.

I was the second kind of treasure. One who had been in service in the 'good old days', when people were 'not afraid of hard work'. I 'knew my place' and never argued with 'my betters' – you name the cliché and it applied to me – or gave the impression of applying to me. That was because the years I had spent in service had imposed upon me a kind of discipline that is impossible to shake off. It was eroded a bit over the years, but when I started doing 'daily' work in 1941, it was still very certainly there. My early impressions were of amazement at the social changes that had taken place in such a short time. To find that these once wealthy families with large staffs were now reduced to a 'daily' two or three times a week! It just didn't seem possible.

I heard various reasons for this – bad management, speculation, but above all taxation. Long and bitter were the diatribes that I listened to about the iniquities of the Chancellor of the Exchequer. To begin with I found it extraordinary that my employers should address me at all on such matters. Money was something that had never been mentioned when I was in service. Perhaps it still wasn't amongst their own class. But it was, it seems, to servants, or to me as a servant, for I was treated to hour upon hour of invective. It amazed me that they thought a member of the working class, and someone who'd been almost *ground down* by their society, should be sympathetic to their cause. But, treasure that I was, I had to seem to sympathize with them – at any rate I made the right kind of noises. Well, I suppose to my mind it was all dead and gone, and what was the point of raking up past animosities? It was a life that would never come back.

One very old and aristocratic lady whom I worked for would regularly tell me that the reason why Britain was no longer glorious was the fault of the Jacks in office, who had *no* tradition of loyalty and no principles. 'It's nothing but one vast middle-class now – the Cult of Mediocrity. Say what you will,' she'd go on, 'say what you will about us, we did have dignity and a sense of responsibility.' But to whom, I wondered? To their King and Country maybe, to their own kind certainly, to the working class rarely. Superficially she and her class blamed the governments for the way their lives had been sabotaged, but as they developed their arguments it was obvious they believed it was with the education of the working classes that the rot had set in. Their position hadn't been challenged until the working classes were educated and became aware that with their skills and their brains they had created a new society which could overthrow the aristocracy. So my old lady and those like her condemned education as being the root of anarchy. She lived in a Beau Geste world of high ideals – and, as she put it, how could anyone who had to grub around for a living – and that meant working for a living – possibly have high ideals?

In my experience she was partly right. When you have to work every minute of the day to provide shelter and food, there isn't much time to think about an idealistic society. So it was that, during my years as a char when I worked with these kind of people, I found that I acted as a sort of catalyst, for when they knew that I'd been a domestic servant, and therefore understood the kind of life to which they'd been accustomed, it seemed to release some sort of well-spring of memories and grievances. They'd talk about the vanished glories of their once-safe world, not because they liked me but because they saw me as their type of working class.

In a way they didn't actually talk *to* me but *at* me. My part in the conversations was to give the appropriate answers. They knew, and they knew I knew, that there could never be any sort of rapport between us, that we each had our recognized station in life, in the same way that we had had when I was below stairs. Let me give an example: the gracious inquiries on a Monday morning as to what kind of a weekend I had had must never be followed up by my asking what sort of a weekend they had had. And when you employ a treasure she understands this. She doesn't feel that she's as good as her employer, or if she does, she hides her opinion, as I did.

Yet I wasn't being hypocritical. I know that, fundamentally, when I was in domestic service I opposed the system, and I have been described as a militant. But I wasn't. I don't think anyone can be militant on their own. At that time, in my situation, militancy would have meant starvation. All I had was an inner feeling that it was all wrong. And of course, events, and by that I mean the general exodus from service, showed that my feelings were justified. But I could never see the point of rubbing the message home to those that I worked for as a treasure (or char). In fact I admired their spirit, that it was able to survive the adversities which had piled on to them – loss of wealth, loss of servants, and above all – and this is what hit them most – the loss of deference which, by reason of birth, they had come to feel was theirs as an inalienable right.

In this book I write about very few of these kind of people, because working for them meant simply a well-ordered home where life went on day after day without change or incident. I had a variety of other jobs, some with people who had no experience of servants but who could now afford help in the home. These people had no tradition of keeping servants, and after a week or two treated you as being on the same social level. There was none of this 'Madam this' and 'Madam that'; they preferred to call me by my Christian name, and many suggested that I called them by theirs. But I didn't care for this too-friendly atmosphere. I've always found that if you get too friendly with your employers it never really works out: they often don't like to ask you to do some unpleasant chore, which annoys them, and then they resent the fact that you've become so friendly and forget they were the ones that encouraged this friendliness in the first place. I always tried to keep it on a 'Mrs' or 'Mr' basis, and for their part they could call me what they liked. I was still a treasure to these people because I would work in with their ideas. If they didn't like these spray-on polishes I was quite happy to use furniture cream, and if they thought that silicone floor polish wouldn't preserve their wooden parquet flooring, then a wax polish suited me just as well. And I was still prepared to get down on my hands and knees and scrub.

It was through these people that I was able to keep fresh and alive my memories of domestic service: they were always so keen to hear about life in the big houses. Elevenses were often taken up by me giving a sort of monologue. They even sometimes asked their friends in to listen to my performance. 'Margaret Powell on the Leisured Classes', one of my employers called it. The Leisured Class. It certainly was that. And I'm reminded of the expression today when I read about the 'problem of leisure for the working class'. What problem? And why is it always assumed that we need guidance to tell us what to do with our spare time? When I worked as a servant for the then leisured class there was no government inquiry as to what my employers should do with their leisure time! They'd have called it unwarrantable interference, as I do now. It seems to me that the country's gone berserk. Recently I read that you could study for a qualification, a sort of Diploma on the Use of Leisure. I thought it was some sort of reporter's joke. Then I read that classes were to be started in the autumn. It's absolutely farcical!

All right, I planned what I should do on my retirement – and planning was part of the fun of looking forward to it. I didn't want anyone else doing it for me. I'm not going to be bored. I've got no problem what to do with my leisure. The trouble is, there isn't enough of it. I still like to remember back to my days as a kitchen maid when my idea of heaven was a place where there was absolutely nothing to do except sit and eat and sleep!

Some readers have written saying that they found *Climbing the Stairs** stronger meat than *Below Stairs** and hinting that perhaps I was following the modern trend of including sex at all costs. This was not the case – nor is it with this book, where some of the meat is stronger still. The point is that *Below Stairs* dealt almost entirely with my early life. When I was young, despite my surroundings, I looked on love and sex as something romantic. I was an avid reader and the writers of the time made it seem that way, so we kept it like that in our conversation and behaviour. Well, of course, there is romance in any lasting relationship and sex is of continuing importance, and it's one thing that the working class have shared in common with all the other classes. At times, though, I've been of the opinion that they thought it was too good for us.

But the power of the working class to survive the hardnesses

* Both available in Pan Books.

of life has been their ability to laugh, not just at misfortune, but at everything that makes up their lives. Their powers of expression are limited and reflect the earthiness of the way they live – but their imaginations are boundless and rich; Balzacian, maybe, but none the worse for that. So that sex and the parts of the body that perform the act have a constant place in their talk, and no matter how they may in fact behave with their husbands or wives, in conversation sex is stripped of any finery.

After I got married and mingled with these kind of people, I found my own attitudes changed. I have never myself used coarse language – not because I'm a prig but because my parents never did, and we were never allowed to at home – but I've learned to understand why most of my class do and to enjoy their company while they are doing it. It is about these people, as well as my employers, that this book is written – so I make no apologies for keeping their idiom.

1

WHEN the war had been on about six months and Albert got shifted from the milk round he was doing to one on the Downham Estate, near Lewisham and Bromley, much to my delight we were offered a council house. It was the very first house we'd lived in since we'd got married – all we'd ever had before was rooms. But the thing that appealed to me most about getting a council house was that it had a lavatory – not only an inside lavatory, but one to myself, and of course Albert. People have said – perhaps it's true – that I've got an obsession about loos, but when you've lived for years in a house with at least three other families and with only one lavatory between you, its use does become a major issue! Not only is it impossible to get out of the loo unobserved, but to get into it at all becomes a very skilful manoeuvre! The last place that we lived in, there were thirteen people, including the children, and only one lavatory between all of us. And we were on the top floor. It hadn't been so bad when we lived on the ground floor because at least it was possible to tell whether the loo was occupied or not, but to come down from the top floor to find it in use and then trying to look nonchalant as you climbed the stairs again, as if it didn't matter whether you used the place or not – well, it was impossible!

There was one place that we were in where the man who lived on the ground floor used to take a deckchair out in the summer and sit right outside the loo. I wasn't so old in those days, and although I wasn't what you would call highly sensitive, I didn't like to ask him to move. If Albert was home I'd get him to ask – he said he 'didn't like talking to the neighbours, let alone asking them to do him a favour'. Do him a favour! I'm sure that was the start of the constipation I suffered from for years afterwards! So perhaps you can imagine my delight at having indoor sanitation and having it all to myself into the bargain. I used to spend a lot of time there. Albert didn't earn very much money and we couldn't afford to use proper toilet paper, so I used to cut up newspaper into neat little squares, thread a string through and hang them on the wall. I learned more about the war from those little squares of newspaper than from anything else!

There was also a garden at the back of our new home. Though it was in an overgrown and derelict state, in my mind's eye I could see Albert converting it into a thing of beauty; a lovely little lawn with a flower bed around it. Because although I'm not a lover of nature when it comes to the wide open spaces, a little bit of garden's another thing entirely.

Mind you, that vision remained in my mind's eye. The main reason was that the soil was solid clay. It was like plasticine, you could make shapes out of it, which some of the neighbourhood children did, and they weren't very nice shapes either. They stuck them on the windows and doors. The other reason was the man next door. He'd made a very good job of his garden – he must have been one of those men with green fingers – but he wanted to stick his fingers into our pie, because whenever Albert went to do a bit of digging, out would come this man and start handing out advice. Now not only was Albert not gregarious, he hated being given advice by anybody. So it was a sort of Box and Cox thing: out would go Albert, out would go old Greenfingers; in would come Albert, in would come Greenfingers. In the end Albert gave up, and it was just as well he did, because very soon the workmen came, dug up half the garden and put in an Anderson air-raid shelter. This was a good thing, too, because no sooner had they finished than the raids started in earnest and it was pretty unpleasant.

We had fifty-seven nights in a row which we spent in the air-raid shelter. Directly it was dark, the sirens went, the searchlights would go on, up would go the anti-aircraft fire and out would come the whole street to run the length of their gardens to get to the Anderson shelters. It used to be a funny sight. To protect themselves from the shrapnel, some would have buckets, or enamel bowls, or even saucepans on their heads. It gave us a feeling of security, but of course, a piece of flak would have sliced through any of them. Night after night as these raids went on I got more and more deathly afraid, though I couldn't show it because of the children – children don't really know fear until they see their elders are afraid. As for Albert, he was a simply marvellous person to be with in a raid. It wasn't that he was consciously brave, it was just that he didn't feel fear. He had got it worked out mathematically that the chances of anything falling on that one tiny little shelter of ours were so remote as not to be worth being afraid about.

The thing that particularly used to worry me was that the railway ran along the end of the garden. In those days there were steam trains with sparks and flames coming from their funnels, and I thought it was the railways the planes were looking for. When a train would stop at the back – it's terribly callous, I know, but I used to long for it to move on and stop at somebody else's back garden – Albert said the planes couldn't see the sparks up there, but I was sure they could.

The only thing that caused Albert any concern, and this wasn't fear, was the incendiary bombs. When these dropped, it meant that he had to get up and do something about putting them out, like shovelling dirt on them or spraying them with a stirrup pump. He hated this, because, as I've said, he wasn't gregarious and this meant consorting with the neighbours, and as he said, he 'hated being pally over a bloody bomb'!

Eventually, even though the raids went on, we stopped using the shelter. It happened this way. The shelter was arranged so that the three boys slept on bunks set about half way up, while Albert and I lay on mattresses on the ground. One morning in the early hours, I woke Albert up and said, 'I'm soaking wet.' 'You can't be,' he said, 'go back to sleep'; then, 'By God, you can be,' he said, 'because I am.' What had happened was that there had been a terrible storm in the night and with the ground being clay, the shelter was flooded. Our mattresses were drenched and we were lying in a pool of water! Right along the gardens we could see people coming out in their night clothes, carrying their children, and calling the weather worse things than they ever did the Germans. When it was light, it was the funniest sight: there on the railings at the end of the gardens were people's bedding and mattresses hanging up to dry. As one of my neighbours said, it looked as if we'd all suddenly become incontinent!

This finished Albert with the shelter. He flatly refused to let us sleep in it any more. We would take a chance and sleep indoors.

We had a large table with cross-pieces of wood underneath, so Albert sawed these off and we put the children to bed under it. I wasn't going to sleep upstairs, so we carried our bed down and put it into the front room. Even then I was still nervous, so I got Albert to take all the doors off upstairs – from the bathroom/loo and the three bedrooms – and we laid these, supported by chairs, over the bed. In fact, if an apple had fallen on the roof, the whole lot would have come down on top of me, but lying in bed and seeing those doors above me made me feel far more safe. The only thing was, we didn't have any privacy using the loo or bathing!

So the raids went on night after night. When I look back on it now, it seems a miracle that we were never hit. There were some pretty terrible incidents around us. One woman with five children was in the shelter at lunch-time and they started whining for their meal. There didn't seem to be any aircraft

13

about so she came out and started giving the kids their food. A bomb fell on the house and killed them all.

Then the house on the corner got hit and was entirely demolished. Fortunately the people were in the shelter. Albert made a fool of himself over this by saying that a bomb never strikes in the same place twice. The following week another one fell on where the house had been and made the crater even bigger.

Then a bomb hit the house opposite: it sliced right down through the kitchen and the stone floor. Again they were all in their shelter. But the bomb didn't explode, so the next morning the wardens came round knocking on every door and we all had to leave in case it went off while the disposal people were trying to get it out.

We didn't know where to go, and then some friends of Albert's said we could live with them. Well, we tried it for three days, but you can imagine it – five of us. They were fed up with us after a couple of days, and we were with them. So we went back to live opposite the unexploded bomb. All this time Albert had to keep going out every morning on his milk round. He had over a thousand customers – all right, he had a horse and cart, but now it wasn't only milk, he had to deliver jam and butter and sugar, and these things were on ration, so all the cards had to be dealt with. I really think that when his calling-up papers came in 1941 he was relieved. I know I was, because married life had got so wretched. He'd come home harassed, depressed and irritable. It was telling on the children – he'd snap at everyone. So, though it may sound heartless, and I'm almost ashamed to say it, I was glad. Mind you, I didn't think they would send him abroad. And they didn't. He joined the RAF. He admits that it was a piece of cake: he did hardly a stroke of work in the four years he was in – rarely saw a plane, never mind about going up in one. He makes me laugh now, because he says he kept them flying. 'Oh,' I say, 'how could you have kept them flying if you never saw any?' He admits to having been the biggest scrounger on the camp, and, as he says, that was saying something!

You may think that I should have sent my sons away, as many other mothers did, under the evacuation scheme, or have

14

gone with them myself. I certainly wouldn't have left Albert on his own, not to do that milk round and to come home to an empty house. I didn't think that anyone would take the three boys together, and I didn't want them separated. I knew they'd be miserable. So we stayed together and, despite everything, I'm glad we did.

I well remember the day Albert went. His sister met us in London to see him off. She was weeping buckets on the platform, and I wasn't. What was the point? He wasn't going into any danger – in fact I was in a lot more danger, left in London with three children.

With Albert gone, I wasn't keen on staying up there, although the raids had now stopped, or were few and far between at any rate. I thought I'd like to get back down to Hove, where my parents were. So I wrote to Mum and said was there any chance of getting a house – to rent, of course, not to buy. She got me a six-roomed house for £1 a week. There was no indoor sanitation, but at least we had an outside loo to ourselves.

The strange thing was that, living down in Hove, I thought the war would seem farther away than it did in London, but this wasn't the case. In fact, as it later turned out, we had more damage done to the house there by the hit-and-run raids, than we had had in London when bombs were being dropped wholesale. The whole seafront was sealed off, and there were so many empty houses. People had left Hove, probably because the raids were *unexpected* – so quick that often the siren didn't go. They weren't trying to bomb the town, because there were no targets. We just got the left-over bombs when they were coming back, or we may have been a sort of training target. Either way, it still wasn't pleasant. So people had left. And even Brighton – a gay town if ever there was one – even Brighton was a dead town.

The house Mum had got me wasn't too bad, but it was inconvenient, because though it was a six-roomed house, it wasn't like our council house, with three rooms on each floor: it had two rooms on three floors, and only one water tap for them all in the basement. It had no bathroom and, as I've said, an outside lavatory. Still, I hadn't really lived long enough in

15

the council house not to be able to adapt myself to a more spartan mode of living.

The house next door was occupied, much to my enjoyment, by an evacuee from London – a Mrs Davis. She had nine children and came from Stepney. I knew a great deal about Stepney through having worked with an under-housemaid, Gladys, who came from there. This Mrs Davis and I got on very well together. Her husband was working in the London Docks. Her children were older than mine: she'd two daughters working in London, two sons in the forces, and the other five were with her in Hove.

Vi, as she asked me to call her when we got friendly, had the most wonderful flow of language – invective, I think you call it. Indeed, her conversation was so liberally interspersed with b's and f's that it was sometimes very difficult to find the original story line in what she was saying. I'm not a prude, as I hope you know by now, but this colourful language did worry me because her children, not surprisingly, caught her complaint and were also b'ing and f'ing all the time, and as my children were playing with them, I had to walk a kind of tightrope between not offending Vi by ever commenting and not letting my sons swear either because I didn't really care for it. Not from them, at any rate. So it was a bit difficult.

Vi was a great favourite in the local pub where all the soldiers came to drink. She was a real scream in there. The soldiers would call out, 'Come on, Vi, tell us another story about married life.' Talk about the Arabian Nights – Vi could have seen a dozen Sultans off. I could write a book of the tales she told, but then, it couldn't be published. The soldiers would keep her well supplied with beer, then someone would say, 'When's the old man coming down?' That was a kind of snide remark addressed to the boy friend of the time who was with her. Old Vi would pipe up, 'Oh, eff him!' Then they'd say, 'Not him, surely he's coming down to eff you!' Talk about Stepney-by-the-Sea! Mind you, Vi used to reckon our local was every bit as good as the one that she used in Stepney. It was a good one, not modernized in any way: plenty of those red plush seats and mahogany bar fittings – it even had spittoons. Not that I saw anyone try to use them. It was a real old-time bar. No music of any kind. The atmosphere was coloured by the conversation and when Vi was there it was blue.

The couple that ran the pub, their names were Flo and Fred; just the right sort – friendly with everybody, whether they drank spirits or beer. They didn't grade their affability towards people by the amount of money they spent there. Flo, especially, was an absolute fund of stories, mostly obscene and unprintable, but in the context of pub life they went down very well – well, after a couple of drinks, I used to think they did, anyway.

Flo was as skinny as a rake and about five-foot-nothing, but nobody took any liberties with her, and she didn't need Fred to protect her from the customers. Her tongue, if any of her customers offended, would change from friendly bawdy tones to neat vitriol. And the unfortunate offender would wish the floor would open up and swallow him. They said they'd once been on a music hall circuit billed as 'Flo and Fred's Frivolities' – they used to show us glossy photographs of them doing their act, him in top hat and tails, carrying a cane, and Flo in a very short skirt. But though I used to go a lot to music halls, I never saw a turn called 'Flo and Fred's Frivolities' – maybe they didn't get any further than the pub circuit, or maybe they were the last turn on the bill, when half of the audience is leaving to avoid standing for the national anthem, and the other half is rushing off to catch the last bus.

When Flo and Fred were in the right mood they'd ask their favourite customers to stay on after closing time. They'd lock the door and do a song-and-dance act for us. Flo, if given enough encouragement in the way of gin, even used to do the can-can! The trouble was she wore those long bloomers with elastic round the bottom – 'passion-killers' they used to call them – so it wasn't exactly authentic, and bore no resemblance to the way they did it in the film *Moulin Rouge*. She used to end by doing the splits. That was even more incongruous. There she sat, legs astride, showing a length of leg and six inches of flesh-coloured knickers. Nevertheless, at her age, it was something to be able to do the can-can at all.

In spite of having five kids there with her, or perhaps because of it, Vi went out every morning doing housework. I used to wonder how she managed to moderate her language and keep the jobs, but as there was a great shortage of that kind of labour at the time, I suppose her employers learnt to put up with it. She'd always come home with something in the way of food, because according to her, people that she worked for used to buy on the black market. This got me envious. At that time I was finding life pretty grim with only the RAF allowance for me and the three kids, so I decided to start going out doing 'daily' work.

I don't know why on earth I decided to work in a vicarage. I must have been a glutton for punishment, as the work there is particularly hard. They were huge places, built when clergy had money and could afford servants, so they were far from labour-saving and since by now most vicars were as poor as their own church mice, there was never any money to spend on them. And a vicarage gets such a lot of wear and tear, what with the meetings of the women's guild and the bible class, the tramping in and out of the boy scouts and the people that hope a clergyman can solve all their problems – it gets like a fairground. Not that I'd ever have gone to my first reverend with any of my problems – not likely. It seemed a most peculiar set-up there to me. Not only did the vicar and his wife not share the same bed, they didn't even share the same floor! For a family, they only had one daughter, about twenty-four years old. I always thought that vicars had a brood of children, that it was part of their duty to get married and have children. If a vicar can't show a big family, the inference is that he got married for the lusts of the flesh. Mind you, all passion must have been spent between those two. It's difficult to lust with a ceiling between you.

It was a different picture when I worked for the Reverend Clydesdale as a kitchen maid. He had nine children, and if the saying is true that it takes a man to make a girl, then the Reverend Clydesdale must have been some man, because he had nine daughters!

Incidentally, the Reverend Clydesdale always had a cup of hot clear soup last thing at night. Mr Wade, the butler, used to serve it to him in his study. One night I said to Mr Wade, 'Why does the Reverend have this hot soup? He has soup at lunch and with his dinner.' 'Oh, there's an answer to that one,' Mr Wade said. 'Have you been in their bedroom?' 'No,' I said, 'I haven't, a kitchen maid doesn't get to look in the bedrooms.' 'Well, over the bed,' he said, 'hang two texts. The one over Mrs Clydesdale's says "Be with me every hour" and the one over the Reverend's "Lord give me strength", and since the Reverend likes to follow the precept of the Lord, by helping those who help themselves, he gives Him a helping hand by swallowing this cup of hot soup every night!' Mind you, as I've intimated, I was never able to prove this since I wasn't allowed in their bedroom.

A funny thing happened on one occasion with this soup because Mrs McIlroy, the cook, had a soft spot for Mr Wade, and she used to pour him a cup of it too, but his she would liberally lace with white wine. One night Mr Wade took the wrong cup upstairs. Well, we thought that would do it, and we quite expected to see Mrs Clydesdale in a certain condition, but even with soup laced with white wine it was too much to ask of him. He was well over seventy-four at the time.

I went to this vicarage three mornings a week, and was given tenpence an hour – not much money for slogging away for three solid hours, and darn hard work it was too. Mrs Goodson was not my idea of a parson's wife. She hennaed her hair, never really getting it the right colour, and plastered herself with make-up. Her favourite expression was 'Blast the parishioners!' The reverend was a man with one or two peculiar habits – I thought they were peculiar. One was that when he knew there was nobody in the house he'd call out, 'Mrs Powell, would you go and see if there's a clean shirt in the airing cupboard for me?' And when I took it into his bedroom, he'd be standing there wearing only his vest and pants. Then he'd try to keep me in conversation. Well, the first two or three times this happened, I thought it must be just coincidence, but as it went on, I knew it was a kind of aberration. Mind you, it did nothing for me, for not only hadn't he the figure that such attire might enhance, I never really regarded clergy as real men – to me they were sort of spiritual eunuchs. Not quite so spiritual, of course, in their vests and pants. Still, when I realized what he was at, I got embarrassed. I don't know why, because on Brighton beach I'd seen men wearing even less than their vests and pants without embarrassment. I suppose it was being in a bedroom, with its connotations of sexual activities. In those days, in ordinary or respectable households at any rate, love-making was confined to what was considered the proper place for such gymnastics, the bedroom. Nowadays, of course, people make love all over the house, or outside come to that. The idea of having a bower sacred to Venus is very out of date today.

Another peculiarity of the vicar's was that when I used to be at the sink washing up, he'd need something from the shelf above it. And as he wasn't very tall, this meant he had to squeeze up against me in order to reach it, and he used to take his time doing it. Now, don't think I'm imagining things. After all, he could have asked me to get it down for him. Nevertheless, I've got to admit that the vicar did work hard at his job as well. If people were too old to come and see him, and they needed help, it didn't matter how far away they lived or what time of the day or night it was, he'd get into his ancient car and chug off to visit them.

By the time I'd been working there about six months I became very friendly with Mrs Goodson – she was an easy sort of person. One day over our elevenses I asked her why she'd married a vicar since she disliked having to join in the church activities so much. 'Oh,' she said, 'he got me on the rebound. I'd been engaged for two years to an officer in the regular Army: we were supposed to be married when he came home on leave from India, but one day I got a letter written in the most flowery language to say that he was head over heels in love with someone out there, and would I release him from our engagement. So,' she said, 'I just took the next man that came along, who happened to be Mr Goodson. I must admit I didn't realize what it entailed, being a vicar's wife. I thought that it was *his* job, not mine as well.' She was bitterly resentful that the Church Commissioners expected her to be as immersed in the parish as the vicar, and I agreed with her. As she said, why should they get two people's work for the price of one? And why, just because she married a clergyman, should she be expected to feel all sweetness and light towards humanity?

20

People expect their food and drink to be dispensed at regular hours, so why shouldn't a vicar have similar hours to dispense spiritual sustenance? Fortunately, she didn't expect an answer to her diatribe. I always had too much to do, and too many financial worries to think much about spiritual matters. I found it enough of a struggle continuing to live in this world, let alone thinking about finding a place in the next.

Although Mrs Goodson was intense, she was gay for a vicar's wife, but not in the sexual sense – she wasn't keen on men at all. Perhaps that was really why she married the vicar – because she thought about them as I did. Anyway, I liked her and we got on fine. She had no 'side' at all, and as for my bit of trouble with the vicar, I got over that by ignoring him when he used to call from the bedroom – he could shout until the cows came home, I just wouldn't answer. And when he came into the kitchen I'd speedily remove myself from the sink. This made him laugh. I said to him one day, 'I don't know how you've got the nerve to get up in the pulpit and tell people how to behave when you're so frivolous yourself.' 'Oh,' he said, 'being a parson's just a job like any other job – I just tell people what they want to hear.' Well, if a full congregation is any indication of a good preacher, he was one. His church was crowded, and that was something, even in those days. Mind you, the war may have had something to do with it, because it seems to me that any threat of a speedy termination of this world makes people think of securing a place in the next!

The reverend's sister Jane also lived with them. She was what you'd call a long-term visitor – she came to stay and forgot to go. She was slightly eccentric in looks and manner. She'd lost her husband in the First World War, her home in the second, and somewhere in middle age she'd lost some of her wits. But with all her eccentricity, she had many endearing ways. She was always kind and gentle, and used to buy people small presents from her stock of clothing coupons. Her most disconcerting habit was walking away from you in the middle of a conversation!

Although Jane was only her sister-in-law, Mrs Goodson was always kind and patient towards her, even when she was being her most irrational. But not so Hilary, the daughter of the house – she was very intolerant. It may have been because her aunt was such a model of fidelity to her lost husband – she had never looked at another man since he'd died and she did rather keep on about it. And, you see, never in this world could Hilary have remained faithful to a lost love, in fact she couldn't to a found one! She was constantly consoling herself for the absence of her husband, who was away in the army, by filling the gap with a collection of men-friends. Hilary's war work was working at an officers' club and also despatching parcels of comforts to the troops, but gossip had it that Hilary dispensed comforts of a much more intimate nature, and the time and the occasion were never lacking.

Hilary was, however, a very attractive woman, adept at the kind of light conversation suitable for dalliance. She joked her way along: during the war, unless you were talking about it, you tried to keep all conversation on a superficial level, and there was an art in it, like playing table tennis – you kept the ball going backwards and forwards. You could talk for an hour without saying anything, yet it was fun and it kept your mind away from the realities of war. Hilary was a master at this verbal ping-pong. So were the officers she brought to the vicarage at frequent intervals. Mind you, they took no notice of me. Some of them, by reason of their birth, were not democratic by nature. And the others, having risen to the officer class, were certainly not going to jeopardize their positions by consorting with a charlady. In any case, the job I was doing there wasn't conducive to sexual badinage. I wore the charlady's uniform of those days, a sort of cotton overall known as a cross-over, and was often down on my knees scrubbing the floors, so neither the dress not the deed made me an object which even the most sex-starved man was likely to cast a roving eye at.

The only officer who came there who ever spoke to me was a Major Baird, a bald, corpulent man. He seemed to me so old that I felt he must be a sort of left-over from the Crimean War, and that, subjected to the rigours of the Russian winters, he'd been frozen into a state of suspended animation. Certainly his conversation had been. I listened for hours about his home in Nottingham, and the 'little woman' that he'd left be-

22

hind. This constant reference to his wife as the 'little woman' made me sort of visualize a tiny ageing woman in a mob cap, but when he eventually showed me a photo of her I had to stifle my mirth – the little woman was broad, buxom, and must have weighed twelve to fourteen stone! Like the major, she carried all before her and it was a matter for conjecture as to how they managed in bed. I commented on this to my friend Vi, and we had an hilarious evening while Vi worked out some half-dozen solutions, the sheer ingenuity of which left me helpless with laughter. When I asked her how she knew these things, Vi said, 'Didn't you ever read that book *101 Things a Bright Girl Can Do*'? Well, I had read a book with that title, but her edition must have been very different from mine!

After I'd been at the vicarage about three months, it was time for Albert to come home on his first leave. He'd been sent to Bridlington to do his square-bashing and most of his letters seemed accounts of the ordeals and tribulations of this strenuous life. How he'd had to stand in the freezing cold wearing only his shorts and a singlet and do a lot of exercises, none of which he could see any sense in, and how, like the Grand Old Duke of York, he was for ever marching up the hill and marching down again. I used to search his letters for the expressions of sentiment that I somehow felt ought to be in them. It was quite in vain. I must admit that we'd seldom used endearing words at home, we just knew we cared about each other and outward expressions didn't therefore seem necessary. But since fate had moved him miles away, I somehow expected him to become very loving and poetic when he wrote, but no, Albert couldn't change.

On the day he was coming home I was like a young bride. I made great preparations – I cooked his favourite dish, steak and kidney pie, and then I spent an hour or so on making myself as glamorous as nature and money would allow. I felt sure that after three or four months' absence – and abstinence, too, I hoped – Albert would certainly want to indulge in some love play. He arrived earlier than I'd anticipated, and I was still in my somewhat scanty underwear – none the worse for that, I thought – and naturally I made a great fuss of him as I sat on his lap waiting for the fireworks to start. Talk about damp squibs. After about five minutes of me sitting there, Albert said, 'Get up, love. I want to clean my boots.' There was a book written after the war, *They Died with their Boots Clean* – Albert nearly did.

After I'd got over my fury, which took some time, what with me feeling rejected and my suspicions that he hadn't been abstinent, we got to talking about it. Albert said that the life was so strenuous, all marching and drilling, that it left no time – or inclination – for amorous interludes. In fact the whole tenor of his life had changed so that he didn't feel the same any more. I thought, this is going to be a marvellous seven days' leave. However, he said he was sure it would come back. Personally, I reckoned that they used to put an anti-aphrodisiac in what they ate or drank to take their minds off it. Vi agreed with me. 'It's the lime juice,' she said, 'otherwise why else do sailors drink so much of it when they're at sea – they never do when they're on shore.' Anyway, whatever the RAF had given Albert wore off as the week wore on, I'm happy to say.

Then it was back to the vicarage and preparations for the church bazaar. You'd never think that such a harmless affair as a church bazaar could cause havoc, and change the lives of so many people.

It was two months before this bazaar was to take place that the Mothers' Union and the Young Wives met in the vicarage to discuss the various stalls and the competitions. It was to be an all-out effort to provide extras for the troops abroad. Most of the members of the Mothers' Union agreed to contribute portions of fat, flour and sugar from their meagre allowance and it was to be my job to make the cakes from their offerings. Various members, particularly those with large families, were giving clothing coupons for material to make cushion covers and such-like. While I don't like to cast aspersions on the vicar's honesty, I was interested to find that his wardrobe was replenished at this time.

I spoke to Vi about this bazaar and she thought she might like to join the Mothers' Union since she didn't know many people down here, but when I told her that it would mean her going to church at least once a week, and that in any case half the mothers were grandmothers, Vi said, 'Not bloody likely.' I breathed a sigh of relief. The thought of introducing Vi and her colourful language to the vicarage had filled me with apprehension. I could imagine her talking at the Mothers' Union about her favourite subject, which was her husband's 'thing'. She was always discussing it. In fact, so much did I hear about it that I felt I knew it as an old friend. I remember the first time I met Alf Davis, my eyes instinctively strayed. According to Vi, Alf's 'thing' failed to perform when he'd had a lot to drink, whereas other men she'd known, they could hardly wait to get home from the pub. And this limpness particularly aggravated her because after a few drinks she used to become very amorous indeed, and certainly needed no urging to get up those stairs! I said to her once, 'You know, perhaps it's just as well the beer affects Alf like that, otherwise you might have had nineteen kids instead of nine.'

The weekend following the church bazaar meeting, two of Vi's daughters came down from London. They were twins, about nineteen or twenty years old, and they had golden hair – natural, too, not bleached. It was a bit of a mystery where that colouring came from, as both Vi and Alf were dark. Vi said they were a throwback, whatever that means. Rosie and Lily were their names: they were very attractive girls. Vi wasn't a bad-looking woman when she troubled to dress up, in spite of having had nine kids and several others that she'd got rid of in embryo.

Lily had brought her boyfriend with her. He was in the fire service, so he hadn't been called up. He was nicknamed Binkie, which I thought rather suspicious, though he probably preferred it to Horace, his real name. After the usual sort of greetings, Vi and I, Binkie and the two daughters all went along to the local. We came back after closing time somewhat riotously, with a couple of Canadians in tow, and all went into Vi's place for more drinks.

Things didn't start off too badly, but I could see that trouble was brewing as the Canadians had eyes only for Rosie and Lily, which caused Binkie to get more and more furious. And of course, the two Canadians were telling tales of the luxury they lived in back home. Although I took it all with a pinch of salt I couldn't call them out since I hadn't the slightest idea of what life was like over there. Brighton and Hove were literally packed with Canadian troops at this time : they all lived on huge ranches, and their families owned thousands of acres of land which they'd wrested from the Indians. No Canadian seemed to have led an ordinary life.

Suddenly Binkie reached boiling point listening to all this talk, and seeing that his Lily was in rapt attention and seemed so enamoured, he shouted, 'You're bloody liars, both of you. Now bugger off before I kick you out!' Rose, whose boyfriend wasn't there, immediately turned round on Binkie and said, 'If there's any buggering off, you'll be the one to do it. After all,' she said, 'these two are over here fighting for our country whereas you went into the fire service so that you wouldn't get called up!' Wow – that did it! Never have I seen or heard such a free-for-all – there was Lily screaming at her sister because of what she had said about her Binkie, and there was Binkie casting the blackest of aspersions on the ancestry of the Canadians, and there was Vi, using every known epithet, trying to break up the fight. I crept out and into my home next door. I quite expected to see the police arriving, but eventually it all quietened down.

The next day when I met Vi, I told her I felt a bit guilty that I hadn't stayed to support her but she said, 'Think nothing of it. You should see some of the fights we've had in Stepney – last night was a picnic compared with them.'

Two or three days before the church bazaar I started making the cakes. I made dozens of small ones for the cake stall and two large ones that I iced, one to be used in a guess-the-weight competition and the other as a prize in the raffle. The bazaar was to be held in the vicarage grounds. The evening before, I went to the vicarage to finish decorating the two large cakes. I left them on the sideboard covered with a sheet of greaseproof paper. I'd done a good job and I felt pleased with myself. You can imagine my horror when I went into the dining-room the next morning and saw that the cat had been eating into them all through the night. They were a travesty.

That was the start of a fiasco of a day. After that calamity followed calamity.

There was a stall called 'objects d'art', and the woman running it asked me over to look at it. She must have noticed the expression on my face. 'Appalling, isn't it?' she said. There were iron holders, antimacassars, stuffed birds, straw mats, beaded bags and cushion covers – which looked as if they'd been made from left-over material from Joseph's coat by somebody who was colour blind. 'Objects' certainly, 'd'art' never. The jumble stall was as bad, with a motley array of old clothes and goods that had been making the rounds of other jumble sales over the years and still had not found buyers! When she saw what she was supposed to sell, the woman who was to run it refused and went home in a tizzy. To add to the chaos, the weather suddenly changed just before the bazaar opened and it poured with rain so everything had to be transferred to the church hall at the bottom of the road. Anybody and everybody helped shift the things, and by the time the stalls were erected in the hall, half of the things were missing. Whoever stole them really must have been in need. It was a sorry, bedraggled affair by the time we got settled. And everywhere there were kids – kids too young to be at school, but not too young to rush around all over the hall screaming at the top of their lungs. The vicar's wife always referred to children as 'raw material'. I saw now what she meant.

Sometimes during these bazaars some form of entertainment was provided. On this particular day there wasn't and it wasn't necessary. Hilary provided all the entertainment that was needed. For some weeks now she'd been going around with a Captain Purcell, an English officer who had some kind of cushy job so that he was allowed to live out, and had taken a furnished flat in Brighton. He'd been to the vicarage a few times and seemed as infatuated with Hilary as she was with him. I didn't much care for him, but then, needless to say, he didn't bother to exert any of his charm on me. He seemed to me one of those men who, insignificant as civilians, suddenly find that with a uniform, and given a small amount of power, they can completely change their personalities. In his own home town he would be just Mr Purcell, living with his wife in a semi-detached-with-garage neighbourhood, growing roses, working in an office all day and living an uneventful life. But there he was Captain Purcell, authoritative, smart, and important to himself. He talked about his men as 'a grand bunch of chaps'. What they referred to him as I never found out, but I could guess.

I don't know whether he and Hilary had been drinking, or whether they just decided to throw caution to the winds. They came into the church hall hand in hand and wandered round gazing into each other's eyes and whispering – sweet nothings, I suppose. Although they were pretending not to look, people's eyes were standing out like organ stops and the tut-tutting that was going on was like machine-gun fire. The loving couple must have been completely oblivious because they sat down in a corner of the hall and started kissing and canoodling. Talk about the Girls' Friendly Society! Their goings-on really brought down the curtain, for after they'd seen their fill, people left in little groups to talk about it. And someone must have done more than talk about it, because the following morning there was a ring at the door. I answered it and there was Mrs Purcell demanding to see the vicar. Hilary was out, in fact she hadn't been home all night. Apparently this someone had found out Mrs Purcell's phone number and told her about the goings-on of the previous afternoon. She'd come down and found her husband and Hilary *in flagranto delicto*, I think it's called. There must have been one hell of a row because, as Mrs Goodson and I listened outside the study door, we heard her say that it was obvious to the parishioners that the vicar had condoned his daughter's behaviour, that she would never give her husband a divorce, and that she was writing to the bishop about the vicar's attitude and behaviour in the matter.

She was as good as her word. The vicar was summoned by the bishop, and because he stood up for his daughter he was removed from his parish and sent somewhere up north. The place buzzed with excitement for weeks. It interested me that the people who talked most about it and visited the sins of the daughter upon her father were those church members who, before, had made so much fuss of him, praising everything he did, calling him Father, and competing for his attention by bringing little gifts which they'd made with their own fair hands. I suppose they'd put him on a pedestal and now he'd fallen off it, they broke their idol into little pieces. For my part, I liked him better. I couldn't help admiring the way he stuck by his daughter, and how he refused to be drawn into any arguments as to the rights and the wrongs of the case.

But it was Mrs Goodson who summed up the whole thing for me and gave me my biggest laugh of the year – 'Fancy,' she said, 'all this fuss over a spot of adultery.'

2

WHEN the vicarage job folded up I naturally had to look for another one. If the children had been older I'd have liked to have got a job on the buses as a bus conductress – they weren't called clippies in those days. But the shift work made the hours too awkward with a young family. I think I would have liked the job because it certainly seemed a lively one, with always somebody to talk to. Of course, the uniform would have done nothing for me, I've never been the right shape to wear trousers. Still, I should have been able to wear them well figuratively speaking, as I'm told I always do. And I'd have enjoyed shouting 'Get up them stairs' twenty times a day! I'd just got to know one of them and she was always saying what a marvellous life it was and what fun she had, but then she was such a pretty girl she'd have had fun in any sort of job. It wouldn't have applied to me! Faces alter cases.

My main reason for wanting to be a conductress was that it would have got me away from doing housework. Because although the houses I went to were far better than mine, the work was very much the same as I was doing at home. Again, being a conductress would have meant that I was in a man's job, and nothing would have pleased me more than to show that I could do it as well as a man, if not better. Vi said that she didn't think I'd have the patience but that wasn't true. I've always had patience if I'm being paid to have it. I've worked for a lot of old dears who weren't pleasant to work for, but I knew they were paying me and I knew I could leave if I wanted to, and while I was there I kept my mouth shut and tried to earn what they were giving me.

But above all, it would have been lively on the buses. The servicemen used them and they were a gay lot when they were off duty, and I'd have met people, which I certainly didn't working in somebody's house or flat. Just the same few faces day after day. Still, it wasn't to be. There was no one to mind the children. But it's an ambition I've had all my life – being a bus conductress – though I didn't realize it then and I most certainly shan't now.

Instead I got a job for one morning a week with a pleasant elderly couple, and although the rate had gone up from ten-pence to 1s 3d an hour and I worked for three hours, this only meant another 3s 9d a week, and didn't make any appreciable difference to my financial state, which was pretty rocky at that time. My three boys were wearing their clothes out as fast as I bought them. I don't know whether not having a father at home made them racket round more, but they seemed to be always wanting new things, or replacements, I should say, be-cause I couldn't afford to buy from shops. I used to haunt the jumble sales. It sounds easy as I write it. Many men chase a ball around on a Saturday afternoon and come back and say they've had a hard game. This is as nothing compared with the rough and tumble of those Saturday jumble sales.

They used to begin at about three o'clock. But by two o'clock there was already a long queue outside, and when the doors used to open it was a free-for-all! A massacre, if you weren't big and strong. Fortunately I was both, so I could elbow my way to the front. Then came the finding and snatch-ing. We were like vultures. In less than half an hour there wouldn't be a thing left worth buying on any of the stalls.

It was through going to a jumble sale that I met Miss Swebert, a lady who I found out later had aspirations to fame. She had a stall for home-made jams – that's what she called them. They were the most appalling things made out of carrots and heaven knows what. Still, in war time anything went. They were just edible, and the boys used to enjoy them.

This Miss Swebert and I got talking and she told me she was looking for someone to come and work for her – two mornings a week, three hours a morning. She was also prepared to pay 1s 3d an hour. This would mean that my earnings would reach the grand total of 11s 3d a week.

Miss Swebert lived on the ground floor of a very large house – there were two floors above – and in exchange for a reduced rent, she was expected to keep the front door and porch clean. Well, the first time I saw this long wide porch and envisaged myself down on my hands and knees scrubbing it, I nearly went back home again!

However, after I'd worked there two or three weeks, and I'd proved myself a *treasure*, I managed to persuade her to let me use a bass broom on the porch. I said the final result would be every bit as good as my getting down on my knees and scrubbing it. I almost convinced myself that it was, but not the upstairs tenants! She had a lot of complaints from them about me using a bass broom – they said the porch was never dry. Well, of course it wasn't as dry as if I'd wiped it with a flannel, but I said, 'There's a war on' – not that that had anything to do with it but it's what everyone said if they didn't want to do something. In any case, by this time Miss Swebert had got to like me so none of the moans from upstairs had any effect on her.

We became very friendly after a week or two and she told me that she was the only child of 'a self-made Yorkshireman'. She showed me a photo of him – self-made he may have been, but he hadn't done a very good job. He was grimness personified. I should imagine she never had any life of her own until her father died. She told me her mother died when she was fifteen, and from that time on any gentlemen friends were forbidden the house. It must have been a grim and cheerless life for her. 'Didn't you ever have a chance to marry and get away from him?' I asked. 'Well,' she said, 'I nearly did, but Daddy' – she still called him Daddy – 'ruined it all. My friend's name was Harold. He was the curate of our church,' she said, 'and we saw each other very frequently because I did the church flowers. One day, with great boldness, I invited him to Sunday tea, and when I told Daddy I thought he'd be furious, but he just said, "I suppose you know what you're doing, you're making a fool of yourself – but let him come." As it turned out I wasn't making a fool of myself. It was Daddy who made a fool out of Harold. Every remark he made Daddy contradicted. He was terribly rude. The meal ended in complete silence. It was dreadful.'

I could imagine the scene. There are some Northerners who pride themselves on 'calling a spade a spade', which is generally a preface to downright rudeness. They call it being blunt. So that, coupled with the characteristics of a Victorian father, this 'bluntness' must have made Miss Swebert's 'Daddy' an absolute ogre to the wretched curate. Yet, considering he must have ruined her life, she was still very loyal to her father. Although it became obvious to me that he had broken her spirit, some people, you know, would have said she was simple-minded. They might have been right, but she was so kind and gentle that I couldn't help liking her, and I'm not and never was a sentimental person by any means. She said from time to time that she felt she would have liked to have been a pastor's wife. I was tempted to tell her about my recent ecclesiastical experiences, but it wouldn't have done with Miss Swebert – everything was kept on a pure plane.

I have said earlier that Miss Swebert had aspirations. They were literary ones. She wrote poetry by the ream, and none of it had ever been published. This didn't surprise me as even I, who at that time had read very little poetry, could tell what awful mush it was! She'd rhyme 'moon' with 'soon' and 'love' with 'above' – that was her type of poetry. Not that I'm against poetry rhyming. I wasn't then and I'm not now, although there's this new way of writing it so that, apart from the way it's set out, it could be prose. Even today I find this puzzling, but then it was downright confusing to me. Miss Swebert was a member of an amateur poetry society called the Melwood Poetry Society. Why Melwood? I wondered. There seemed no connotations and nothing poetic about Melwood. It appeared that the name came from the founder, who was a Mrs Amelia Ross Wood; it was a sort of amalgam of her Christian name and her surname.

This Mrs Ross Wood's grandmother, or great-grandmother,

I forget which, had been a cousin of Thackeray's and this was her claim to literary fame, and she certainly played on it! She had all Thackeray's books, everything he'd written – leatherbound and gold tooled – very prominently displayed in her drawing-room. Also I learned from Miss Swebert that she'd been named Amelia after the heroine of *Vanity Fair*, though again I gathered she bore no resemblance to that Amelia who, from reading the book, I remembered as a wishy-washy sort of person who wept at the slightest provocation. My heroine in *Vanity Fair* was Becky Sharp – I should have enjoyed making the same mistakes as she did.

The Melwood Poetry Society had apparently started with about twenty members, but owing to the air raids twelve of them had departed to live in a safer climate, where their cultural gifts were in no danger of being cut off before they reached their prime. I'd always heard that poets enjoyed suffering! Those that were left, as I found out later, were elderly; three widows, two spinsters and three with nondescript husbands who enjoyed being fussed over when they attended the meetings.

When Miss Swebert and I had our elevenses, and we had them together – there was none of this business of her leaving my cup in the kitchen while she took hers into the lounge – she used to read her poems to me, and sometimes she wanted a bit of advice on those she hadn't finished. Although I was hard put to it not to dissolve into laughter at the high-falutin' sentiments they expressed, I just couldn't hurt her feelings – it would have been like ill-treating a child. Anyway, I was a bit flattered, so I'd keep a straight face and discuss them as though they really had some hopes of being published.

Then one morning she said to me, 'You know, Mrs Powell,' she said, 'you seem so interested in poetry, perhaps you would like to join our Society?' Well, nothing was further from my thoughts or my wishes. It was bad enough having to sit there and listen to her spouting away. Still, I looked at it like this: all the time I was listening to her, I wasn't doing housework. It was a bit of cake, that job.'How much does it cost?' I said, hoping to get out of it that way. 'Oh, never mind about that,' she said, 'I'll pay the membership fee.' So, well, although I was all set to refuse once again, I just couldn't hurt her. And let me be honest – such is human nature that vanity had once again crept into it. The very thought of belonging to a poetry society – a charlady on a par with people who *pay* to have charladies – this was one-upmanship. So I said, hypocrite that I was, 'How kind of you, Miss Swebert – I'd love it.' I don't know why the words didn't choke me.

When I went to the first meeting Mrs Ross Wood didn't approve of me at all and she showed it. I tried to ingratiate myself with her by letting her know that not only had I read *Vanity Fair*, but many other Thackeray books, and indeed I had. You'd have thought that this would have endeared me to her, as she was a descendant of Thackeray. But not on your life! In fact, I think it seemed an affront to her that a charlady should read at all! She reminded me in that way of Lady Downhall, for whom I was cook, and when I asked if I might borrow a book from her library, said, 'Oh, certainly, Margaret, you may – but I didn't know you *read*!'

Despite Mrs Ross Wood's antipathy towards me, the meeting went on, and during it I discovered that the members were all going to enter a poetry competition held annually by some obscure magazine. It was advertised in the personal column of *The Times* – you sent them your poetry and they paid you for it if it was published, and the winning poem got an additional prize of £5.

All the members were very much in earnest about their contributions. To me it seemed incongruous. I sat there thinking about the foulness of the war and how there were these members writing and spouting out this mushy stuff, you know, about Love and Devotion, and the contrast made me furious at the time. Why I don't know. The war wasn't their fault, but it was just that I felt nothing serious had ever touched their lives. Since then I've learned how wrong I was – you can't tell with people. Some of those who, outwardly, are the most serene, have had most tragic lives.

But the poetry society wasn't all hearts and flowers. Mrs Ross Wood had written what she called an 'elegy', although to my mind it bore no resemblance whatsoever to the only elegy that I knew, Gray's one on the churchyard. Still, hers was certainly mournful, and I had a strong suspicion that chunks of Tennyson's *Mariana* were included in it. She had a lot of words like 'dreary' and 'weary', which reminded me of *Mariana*, and I'm not showing off when I make the comparison. I know about it because it was drummed into me at school. Fancy giving children that poem: there was this Mariana continually sighing and moaning – I remember thinking what a drip she must have been! I'd never read it since, but I was sure Mrs Ross Wood had lifted chunks out of it.

Miss Swebert, of course, had written her usual stuff addressed to the moon. But I didn't think it was too bad – a bit sentimental, but it was one of her best efforts.

Of course, she persuaded me to enter this competition – not that I needed much persuasion, being convinced by this time that I could write as good poetry as anything they were turning out. So I set to, and got my bit done. I remember reading it to my sons. I was subjected to hoots of derision, but I put it all down to their ignorance. Mind you, I never dared go next door and recite it to my friend Vi – she'd have simply died of laughing if I had! I was, as it were, leading a double life at the time.

My contribution was a piece on mental illness – about suicide. I thought that it had the merit of at least being different, and it was all my own work, which was more than could be said of many of the other members, much of whose efforts, like Mrs Ross Wood's, had been lifted. Ignorant as I was, the contrast between the good and bad lines was so marked that I or anyone else would have noticed the plagiarisms.

Of course, at the meetings everybody praised everyone else's poems. I've always found that, with any amateur group, they always turn out to be a sort of mutual admiration society. They even said mine was good. Eventually the poems were sent off: then came the weeks of waiting. As the time went on I became sure that I'd be the winner and I'd spend the money in my imagination in setting the children up with clothes that would last them for months and months.

Eventually we got back our copies and, needless to say, I hadn't won: written on mine was *Shows Promise*. This didn't mean anything at all – everybody 'showed promise'. Everybody, that is, except Miss Swebert – she was *Very Highly Commended*, and this delighted her and delighted me, and it was one in the eye for Mrs Ross Wood.

Now when I look back on it, I reckon it was all a swindle. It cost five shillings to enter, so the organizers were on to a good thing when you think about it. They didn't give the name of the prize winner, so nobody could check up. It was probably just a con trick; but who cares – it gave many people a lot of fun.

Shortly after this, my association with Miss Swebert ended in a sad way. An old aunt of hers in Cheltenham wrote to ask if she would go and live there and look after her, and Miss Swebert had such a strong sense of family duty that she felt she should do this. I tried to persuade her against it, but she would go. In a way, I admired her for it, but I was sorry because I lost a good job and a friend. Not many of the people I've worked for have I really liked, but I was very fond of Miss Swebert. The end of our relationship was so ironical. I corresponded with her regularly after she left. Then, after about two months, I had a letter from her aunt, who wrote, 'Dear Mrs Powell, My niece thought so much of you that I'm sure you will be very sorry to hear that she was knocked down by a car last week and killed instantly.' She went on to say, 'I am enclosing a brooch of hers that I thought you would like to have as a remembrance of her.' When I read this letter I felt a sense of *fury* with life, at the illogicality and unjustness of it, that such a kind and inoffensive person should die like that. She had left a town where air raids were a constant hazard, to live in what was known then as a 'safe' place. To lose her life by what was then a minor hazard, in war time, and because of her sense of duty to an ailing relation seemed so unjust.

I was very grieved for a long time but it was some comfort to think that she was spared a lonely old age.

3

IT was a strange coincidence that when my job with Miss Swebert ended I also lost my one morning a week with the elderly couple I was working for, since they decided to sell their house and move into a cottage in the country. There was some talk of me going with them; how there was a place nearby which would suit me and how I could then 'do' for them full time. But dear me, no – I'm not a nature lover. I've never been one since I was very young and my parents used to take us on outings into the country. I had an inferiority complex which increased the further we got away from the town. I think the country diminishes you. There you are, looking at things that have been around from time immemorial, and whether they got there through some Greater Power like God or whether they came out of the Void, there they are, unchanged, and you know that when you've gone they'll still be there. But the marvels of the town are made by man alone – and this, to me, enhances his importance. All right, they may not last, but when they go, man will have invented something even better to take their place. In the town anybody is somebody. In the country we're just part of the scenery.

So, for all the talk, I wouldn't have dreamt of going into the country to work for them. But the fact that two employers were giving up their houses was of considerable benefit to me, because they gave me quite a lot of their surplus furniture, and we needed it very badly. Prior to the war, we never had more than three rooms, and now we had this six-roomed house, and with the war on and the lack of money and everything on coupons, we'd got very little furniture in each room. At this time I was looking for another house to rent, partly because with two rooms on three floors and the only tap in the house in the basement, I was constantly running up and down stairs, and partly because I had now fallen out with Vi over her children's swearing. My boys had picked up the habit through playing with them, and they used to come out with the most terrible expressions, which didn't pass unnoticed at their school, so I was asked to do something about it. Moving seemed the only way out.

I must have looked at dozens of houses to rent – and there were plenty because nobody was keen on living in Brighton or Hove because of the air raids. Most of those that I looked at weren't fit for animals to live in: the floorboards were rotten and they reeked of damp. In one place I saw, there was fungus growing on the inside walls! After a deal of searching I thought I'd found somewhere that wasn't too damp or decrepit, but when I climbed up into the loft there was a pile of old mattresses. I turned one of them over and saw they were full of bugs. It wouldn't have been so bad if they had been fleas. Fleas at that time were an occupational hazard, but with bugs you have to remove all the skirting boards and woodwork to fumigate the place to get rid of them, and even then their demise is problematical!

Eventually I did find a house, at £1 a week, the same rent I'd been paying. It was a two-storey building with a beautiful attic – of course, there was no bathroom or inside lavatory. As Albert was due for another leave at this time, he was able to help me to move. Mind you, I wondered whether he'd have the strength, as two months before he'd been moved to a camp where he and another chap were the only two men among over a hundred of the Women's Auxiliary Air Force. I remember him writing and saying he felt like a sultan. I didn't feel in the least bit alarmed. I thought that there was a kind of safety in those sort of numbers. Mind you, when the day came for him to arrive on leave, I didn't bother to make myself look glamorous this time – I couldn't hope to compete with such a bevy of females! I've often wondered since about this safety in numbers bit because when his leave was up he didn't show any reluctance about returning. Perhaps it was imagination on my part, or can it have been that one woman and three kids, the house all upside down with the moving, and the bitter cold couldn't weigh in the balance against a warm cookhouse with over a hundred females cavorting around?

After Albert went back, I got another morning job and again the rate of pay had gone up – it was 1s 9d an hour now. It seemed fantastic that every time I wanted another job I found the money had increased. This job was for a Mr and Mrs Wilson – a youngish couple in their early thirties. When Mrs Wilson found that I had been in what I could now call professional domestic service, she welcomed me with open arms, and I hadn't been there more than a month before she raised my money to the unheard of sum of 2s 6d an hour! She said I was worth every penny of it – an absolute treasure!

This increase of money had never happened to me before – nor has it happened since. Why wait until your workers are screaming for more pay and are dissastified before giving them what they deserve and what you can afford? However, so many of the people I worked for were on fixed incomes. For them the cost of living went up and up and their incomes didn't increase to meet it. I wouldn't have dreamt of asking them for more money because theirs became a hard life. It is hard, when you've been used to certain standards, to keep having to lower them. Brighton and Hove have housed many of the decaying gentry, some of whom I hated in my early days in service, but the like of whom I've since learned to pity.

Mr and Mrs Wilson weren't hard up, nor were they of the gentility – they both went out to work. He was in a reserved occupation, something to do with aircraft, and she worked in a factory, and between them they made more money than they were able to spend. In war time, with everything on ration and with no luxury goods in the shops, there was a limit to what you could buy. Of course, there was the black market; to which I was one of the providers, because I'd sell my clothing coupons for money to pay for food, though this had its limitations and its risks.

Financially, and in many other ways, this was a good job. The only real snag, and it was a major one, was that Mr and Mrs Wilson quarrelled violently. So much so that I dreaded the mornings when they were home together. They both worked on shifts, and occasionally their times coincided. They would quarrel about anything and everything, and the fact that I was there made no difference to them. Indeed, often they asked me to arbitrate, but I never would. I learnt very early in life that nobody loves an arbitrator – not even his mother. Rows have always frightened me; I suppose because I'd not

39

been used to them either in my own home or when I was in domestic service, as Them Upstairs would never knowingly demean themselves by quarrelling in front of the servants. The Wilsons had never been and could never be of the kind of Them Upstairs. They weren't, like me, of the working class, they were lower middle class with a middle-class income. This was reflected in their attitude towards me. But this quarrelling used to get on my nerves, and I'd feel embarrassed because the most intimate details of their married life used to come out.

It was always the same pattern: the row would start over some small thing and end with each calling the other sexually inadequate. I suppose when you quarrel in bulk, detail ceases to have any cutting edge, and only by imputing lack of virility to each other can you hope to wound. I mean, tell a woman she's a terrible housewife and she may well agree, but suggest that she wouldn't attract a drunken sailor and she'll have your guts for garters!

Mr Wilson was a man who was very unsure of himself. Not of his work, he knew he was good at that, but unsure socially and particularly where the opposite sex were concerned. I felt that he got married because he couldn't prove that he was a man until he did, and having married, he didn't like its permanency. What he wanted was money and success, but he equated these things with happiness, and when they didn't provide happiness he became embittered, and his bitterness was the basis of these quarrels.

When he was at home on his own in the mornings I was always faintly uneasy. He had an obsession about physical fitness and he was always doing exercises, just wearing a pair of swimming trunks. There was a spare room there and he had had this equipped with keep-fit gadgets: pulleys and springs and a sort of pedal machine for exercising his leg muscles. He used to spend an hour a day at this you-too-can-have-a-body-like-mine activity. To see him walking around in trunks always made me feel a bit quaint. I remember when I first saw him like it, I thought it might be a prelude to an amorous interlude during the elevenses. I either did him an injustice or over-estimated my sexual attractions, because he never showed the slightest interest in me. And such is the perversity of woman that I felt quite peeved about it. Had he laid a finger on me I should have gone into the routine of shocked resistance. What I really wanted was for him to look at me with eyes blazing with desire yet to do nothing about it. But of course, any man that looks like that swoops. Many a swooper I've had to combat in my time.

I remember wondering why Mr Wilson did all this keep-fit lark. After all, with him not being in uniform, I thought that he wouldn't have wanted to look the picture of health, otherwise people would think he was dodging the call-up. In that war, though, fanatical females didn't go round giving white feathers to men out of uniform as they did in the 1914 war. I remember then (I must have been about nine or ten at the time) seeing a group of young women trying to give a man a white feather. He protested and tried to get away from them, and a crowd gathered and he got roughly treated, and eventually the police came and protected him. I got very upset about it – I didn't know the pros and cons but I didn't like seeing him set on in this way, and I went home crying to my mother. She was naturally interested so she bought the evening paper and there was a report about it, and it turned out that the reason the man wasn't in the army was because he had a weak heart, and that he'd got the weak heart some years before when he'd tried to save a little girl from drowning.

I've often thought about the difference in attitude towards men out of uniform in the two wars. In the first one I believe that the reason people were so fanatically patriotic was because they were not involved – all right, their husbands, sons, brother or sweethearts had gone, but they themselves knew little of the foulness of war. There were the odd zeppelin raids, they walked around in a semi-blackout, and they were short of a few things, but they didn't actually suffer physically. In the last war the full force was visited on the civilian population. There was as much heroism from people out of uniform as from those in it, and we were conscious of this and because we were all involved we were more considerate and understanding towards each other. Or mostly all, except people like Mr and Mrs Wilson, who were always at each other's throats!

Apart from this keep-fit mania Mr Wilson had another

hobby – collecting toy soldiers. He had all kinds, right back to bowmen and knights in shining armour. Real lead they were, not the plastic things they make nowadays.

On the mornings when he was at home, he would draw them up in battle array on the dining-room table, working out the strategy for imaginary battles. It seemed a footling occupation to me. I'd heard of armchair generals, but they were men who had once been in command in the services and were now reliving their days of glory, while Mr Wilson had never fought a battle in his life, except with his wife, and he never showed any enthusiasm for giving up his well-paid job to try the real thing.

Mind you, I noticed that he never fought *modern* wars, and when I asked him why, he went off into a long rigmarole about old-time fighting being very different from the foul way it was done now. According to him, chivalry abounded in days gone by and the weapons were nicer. But I couldn't see that it was better to be killed by an arrow, a sword or a cannonball than any other way. And as for chivalry, I used to point out to him that the Crusades, although they were ostensibly religious wars, were crueller and bloodier than most, and that the atrocities were committed just as much by the Christians as by the Turks. It seems to me religion can bring out the worst as well as the best and I got sick to death of hearing about righteous wars, with both sides going to church and praying that God will send them victory, while they're killing, shooting, maiming and torturing. The bloodiest wars of all wars are described in the Old Testament, many of them ending up with the Israelites counting the number of foreskins they'd cut off the Philistines. Those Israelites were bestial and downright unhygienic.

So, what with his keep-fit exercises and his toy soldiers, Mr Wilson wasn't *my* idea of a man. In spite of his virility, his money and his undoubted good looks, I didn't envy Mrs Wilson her life with him. His fiery temper would have fed me up long ago. I must admit, though, she could give as good as she got when it came to a slanging match. I just couldn't understand a couple living together in a state of permanent warfare. But maybe they got a sort of kinky pleasure out of it.

Perhaps it was a kind of excitement for them, culminating in a big reunion when they went to bed at night. Many people, I believe, who've had terrible rows in the day try to keep them up so that they can have the grand reconciliation at night. That sort of thing would never have worked with Albert and me, partly because he won't argue and partly because no matter how irate I become, he just goes off to sleep!

One of the things the Wilsons were always on about was that he wouldn't let her have a child. He disliked all children. One of the reasons he gave was that he was one of thirteen and had had a rotten childhood; so he wasn't going to have his wife breeding like a rabbit. But, as she said, having one child could scarcely be considered breeding like a rabbit. Then he'd go on to say that she knew when she married him that he didn't want a family, so he hadn't cheated her. But of course, like so many brides-to-be, she thought that once they were married, she could change him. It's funny, isn't it, how so many wives want a different man once they're legally bound? You can't help wondering why they didn't choose the right one to start with.

I was just the same at the beginning of our married life with Albert. It wasn't that I wanted more money or possessions – those sort of things never worried me – but I wanted him to get on, to be more ambitious, but when I saw it worried him I stopped because I don't think any woman has the right to upset a man in that way. But we do try to make a man over, and he has a right to be annoyed when you come to think about it. After all, his mum and dad and his friends have liked him as he was – and he assumes that the female who takes him on must like him for what he is, otherwise why did she marry him? Then the alteration process starts, and he suddenly finds he's not the man he thought he was. It must be very disconcerting, if not downright disillusioning.

I did make Albert over in some ways, and I don't apologize for it. I remember his mum coming one day to lunch (or dinner, as we call it, because like all working-class people we have dinner at lunch time and tea at night) and after the meal was over, she sat down, I washed up and Albert wiped, and she said, 'Oh, he never did anything like that for me when he was at home!' 'No,' I said, 'I don't suppose he did, but men do many more things for their wives than ever they do for their mothers.'

Anyway, back to Mr Wilson and the way he kept his home clear of any encumbrances. He wouldn't even have a dog. And here I was able to agree with him. I don't think a town is the place for dogs. I think they're fine in the country but they're trespassers in towns. They foul the pavements and, despite the laws, their owners deliberately let them do it. They're a nuisance in pubs, on the lead or off. I was in one recently where a woman let her poodle off the lead and it ran and jumped on every single chair. And the times I've been messed around by dogs on buses! Some years ago in Brighton and Hove you didn't have to pay a fare for them. Then one was introduced. And the protests! You'd have thought that children were being deprived. A petition was started and one woman came to my door. 'What's it about?' I said. 'It's a protest against paying a fare on public transport for dogs.' 'You've come to the wrong house,' I said. 'I'll sign one if it's for paying double fare for dogs!' I know the British are a nation of animal lovers, but I'm all for keeping things in their place and in their proper perspective.

I remember being on top of a bus, and the only seat vacant was by a woman who had her dog sitting on it. I stood there for a bit and she lifted up the dog and put him on her lap. I kept standing. Then she said, 'There's a seat,' and I said, 'I don't care to sit where a dog's been.' She got indignant. 'The dog's perfectly clean!' 'How can it be?' I said. 'It's got four feet that've been walking around on the ground. No, you get up and sit where the dog's been and I'll sit where you are!' I didn't get a bit of sympathy or agreement from my fellow passengers. Just the opposite. If looks could have killed!

But Mr Wilson liked cats and they'd got a female one, and like all female cats it was always having kittens, and in the most unexpected places. I mean, who'd have thought that this one would have chosen one of Mr Wilson's boxes of toy soldiers? Mind you, he kept them wrapped up in cotton wool, so it was a soft bed. When he found out, I thought the roof would have blown off!

Another of Mr Wilson's less desirable traits was not only his inability to laugh at himself but his complete lack of any sense of humour or sense of fun. If he ever heard Mrs Wilson and me laughing together he'd come into the room looking very suspicious – I think he thought we were laughing at him.

Anyway, despite the way his soldiers had been violated the cat was allowed to live and they even kept one of the kittens.

One Friday morning when I went to work, Mrs Wilson told me they were going into the country for the weekend, and would I look in Saturday and Sunday to feed the cat and kitten. I agreed to do this, and when I went in on the following Monday, I quite expected them to be in good form after a change from the old routine. Much to my surprise, I found Mr Wilson was in bed, somewhat indisposed. I asked what was the matter with him, but Mrs Wilson was too overcome at first to tell me – not with grief but with laughter. She manoeuvred me into the kitchen and shut the door so that he shouldn't hear.

She told me that they went to stay at an inn where they'd spent their honeymoon. On the Friday evening and Saturday morning everything was fine, but on Saturday evening they both drank too much and eventually had a terrific quarrel. He marched off into the night at about ten o'clock. By eleven, when he hadn't returned, she decided to go and look for him. As she was walking along the country lanes carrying a torch, a lorry drew up and the driver offered her a lift. As the man was elderly, she felt it was all right and accepted. After about two miles she saw Mr Wilson walking by the side of the road. The driver stopped and she got out, but when she turned to greet Mr Wilson he'd vanished. As she said, she couldn't believe it because the road was straight and, with the torch, she could see a fair distance. She said, 'I stood there, wondering what to do, when suddenly a figure seemed to come up from the ground in front of me.' It was Mr Wilson. It appeared he'd stepped aside to avoid the lorry and being still somewhat drunk, over-balanced and fell into the ditch. As she flashed the torch on him, she screamed, for he seemed to be covered in blood. He wasn't, it was just that the ditch he'd fallen into was full of red mud and he was covered in it. She said he looked like her grandfather did when he came back from work. He was a ruddle man in the north country. A ruddle man was one who went round selling the red ochre which people used on their steps if they didn't hearthstone them. He had to quarry it and prepare it himself, and by doing this year after year, it penetrated into his skin so that he became red. So there was Mr Wilson standing before her, the very picture of her grandfather – the ruddle man! The lorry driver gave them a lift back to the inn. He didn't speak a word to either of them. He must by now have thought he'd got into some sort of lunatic world and the sooner he was shot of them the better.

After she told me this story, I said, 'But what's this got to do with him staying in bed? Did he catch a cold?' 'Oh no!' she said, and went off into peals of mirth. 'No, it's not that. We came back here on Sunday, he was still furious with me and I was furious because he was furious, and nagged at him all the way. When we got into bed we had another flaming row. I told him he was no bloody good round the house; that the sash cords had been broken for months, the lamp in the bedroom wouldn't work and the pipe under the sink was *still* leaking. With that,' she said, 'he leapt out of bed and said, "Oh well, I'll fix that bugger now. Then perhaps you'll shut up!" Well,' she said, 'as you know, he sleeps in the nude.' This didn't mean what it sounds like. She knew that I'd know because I made the bed and there were never any pyjamas to fold. Anyway, he'd once said to me that going to bed in your pyjamas was like sleeping with your socks on, whatever that was supposed to mean. So I just nodded and she went on with the story.

'He jumped out of bed naked as the day he was born,' she said, 'and rushed into the kitchen. I heard him slam open the drawers to get the pliers to unscrew the pipe. There was a bit of grinding as he tried to loosen it – then a scream, a thud, a bump and a miaow. I rushed into the kitchen and found him lying on the floor with one hand on his head and the other between his legs, moaning. I was full of sympathy. I got him back to bed and he told me what had happened. As he went into the kitchen he must have woken the kitten and when he stooped down under the sink, it was curious to know what was going on. Then when it saw the thing between his legs dangling to and fro, it must have thought, "That's something

46

peculiar," because it pounced at it and hung on with its claws.

'Well, this caused him some pain and some shock. He tried to jump up, hit his head on the sink and fell back half conscious onto the floor, where I found him, and now he's in bed with bandages on both the places that were injured. Go and ask him to show them to you!'

Well, of course, this sent us both off into screams of laughter. The thought of Mr Wilson, who was so proud of his physique, lying there with a bandage on the most important part of it was too much for me. I was nearly in hysterics. He must have heard us because beyond saying good morning to me, he hardly ever spoke to me after that. It was rather uncomfortable for a long time. Still, it was worth it. Talk about Kitchen Sink Drama! I laugh even today when I think of it. Poor Mr Wilson!

It was now early in 1944, and I thought I might be able to give up going to work. Albert had been promoted to a Leading Aircraftsman and had written to say he was going on a course which, if he passed, meant he would become a military policeman, a red cap, and he would get more money. However, shortly afterwards, he sent another letter and said he had discovered that if he became a policeman he wouldn't have any friends so, although he'd got to go on the course, he'd make sure he didn't pass. I wrote back and agreed with him. Under those circumstances it was better I should go on working. So I decided to stick at the Wilsons'.

Although relations with Mr Wilson were a bit strained, Mrs Wilson was very friendly, and she raised my wages again, without my asking. I was now getting 2s 9d an hour, which was well over the average daily rate.

It wasn't only the money. I liked working with her because, although better off than me, she hadn't any side and I could always keep my end up with her. Sometimes we used to go out together. I remember once we went to a meeting of the Brighton and Hove branch of the Anglo-Russian Fellowship. It was a sort of Aid to Russia Society. The speaker was an MP – a Mr Horobin. I don't remember what he said, but what I do remember was that there was a collection for the Russians and all I had on me was thruppence! Other people gave at least half-a-crown, and the horrible thing was, there wasn't a bag to put the money in, it was a flat plate, so everybody could see what I gave. I felt so mortified about my thruppence – I wasn't upset that I couldn't help Russia, but those three coppers rattled as I put them down and I felt that every eye in the place was focused on me.

It was all malarky, wasn't it, this helping Russia? I'm not just being wise after the event. I knew even then that we were only helping them because they were helping us, and it wouldn't be long before we stopped looking at Russia as our Glorious Ally. It had been the same after the First World War; came the Revolution, we didn't want to know, we wouldn't give them house room. We were all for the aristocracy and we didn't care about the poor. Not that I'm a Communist – far from it. I'm a realist. I've always had to be.

Mrs Wilson felt the same way about the Anglo-Russian Fellowship, but it didn't stop us from going to other meetings. We were gluttons for punishment. For example, there was a Make Do and Mend Week at one of the large stores in Hove. Why I bothered to go I don't know – I'd been making do and mending for years! I think Mrs Wilson had visions of becoming a model housewife, and perhaps repairing relations with her husband, him having less cause to quarrel. To my mind, the essential skill that she needed to learn to stop him from doing this was cooking. I agreed with Mr Wilson when he said the only decent food he ate was when he had meals out.

My misgivings were right, because at this Make Do and Mend there was some high falutin' lady giving the talk, and it was obvious that she had a large wardrobe of expensive clothes to make do with. Enough to see her through two world wars. So there we were, listening to her talking about silks and satins when I was thinking in terms of cotton and flannel. The kind of clothes that most of us there had, had probably been mended so many times that the material wouldn't lend itself to Making Do in any case! Still, I was a lot luckier than many people. Those that I worked for gave me some of their old things, as well as bits of food that helped to eke out the rations and the money. As a family we survived the war. We were all in good health, had had many a laugh, but although I was glad when the war was over, I also realized that, on Albert's return, I was going to have to sacrifice a sort of freedom of action that I'd got used to and that this wasn't going to be easy.

4

IN November 1945, Albert was demobbed and came back home with a small gratuity and a demob suit which looked like it sounds.

I remember even now quite vividly those first few months with a man about the house again. As I've already said, I realized that a lot of adjustment would be needed, and I found it very hard to relinquish the reins of authority after four years. I'd enjoyed making all the decisions and being the one to be consulted by the boys about their problems. I'm sure I wasn't alone in this. It must have been the same in many families, probably with far greater discord than in ours. Albert was – and still is – an easy-going man, and he made this period of readjustment easier for me than it might have been.

But it was still a problem to be tied down to regular meal times, doing the things that he was going to like done, having to ask for my share of the wage packet and not getting my money from the government any more. When you've once been the general, it's not nearly so much fun being a lieutenant. It wasn't for me, anyway.

Our immediate problem was what was Albert going to do? His work had always been in London before the war. He'd worked for the Express Dairy and, though they offered him his old job back, with an increase in wages, we couldn't get anywhere to live in London. Unfortunately the Express Dairy didn't operate in Brighton and Hove, and though he might have been employed by a local milk firm, he was a bit obstinate, as men sometimes are, and said if he couldn't work for the Express Dairy he wouldn't be a milkman. I didn't blame him. After the cushy life he'd had in the RAF he'd have found it a mighty gruelling job. Mind you, even if we could have got a house I hadn't the slightest desire to go back to London. It's all right being up there if you've got enough money to live in the right places, but some of the dingy areas are not like London at all. Not the London we sing about, anyway. They might be anywhere with their rows of mean little houses shared by two or three families, with just a dusty park for the children to go to.

Then there was the boys' education. They were all doing so well at school, it would have been a sin to move them. And, of course, we were still only paying £1 a week for our house – which, while it could never be called 'Sea View' except by a crooked boarding-house keeper, did get the benefit of the sea air.

Albert wasn't too pleased at not going back. He couldn't bear living by the seaside because of the sea breezes. In those days Albert wore a trilby hat, and for most of the year it was impossible to keep any sort of hat on unless it was a Bill Sykes cap. And there's always been a touch of the fop about Albert. He'd never wear a cap. He didn't like the sea and he doesn't now. He never walks along the promenade except once a year, on August Bank Holiday, and that's the day it becomes London-by-the-Sea with the influx of day-trippers. I suppose Albert's what you'd call a real Londoner. He's never been one to sit on the beach exposing his torso to all and sundry and, with or without a hat, there's one thing that he hates, and that's the wind. I used to tell him how bracing it was for him. 'Yes,' he'd say, 'sometimes I've been so braced it's taken me a week off work to recover from it!'

Anyway, since it was virtually impossible for us to go back to London, he'd got to settle for a job where we were. So he went along to the local Labour Exchange and, since he was classed as unskilled, having been a milkman, there weren't many jobs available. I don't see why a milkman should be classed as unskilled. Pushing a milk barrow around the streets may not require any, but there's a lot of mental skills needed to soothe irate customers if you've overcharged them or forgotten to leave the right milk! Albert was marvellous at it. He could convince a customer whom he'd stuck two or three pints on in a week that he was really undercharging her. Then there was the business of getting the money out of people. This was a fine art as well as requiring a high moral sense.

When he was on his rounds in Maida Vale, many of his customers were in bed, because in those days a lot of prostitutes plied in that area – I don't know whether they still do – and since it is mainly night work, they used to sleep on in the mornings; so when they answered the door they'd be in their flimsies, and some of them used to ask him to take it out in trade! Talk about the temptations of Faust! He told me he always refused, but I don't know – he used to come home pretty tired sometimes! So, as I say, I reckon it was a highly skilled occupation taking it all in all.

The only two jobs that Albert was offered were being a stoker at the gasworks in Portslade, which was at one end of the town, or being a furniture remover at the other end. And it was his hatred of the wind that decided his future destiny, because he went after the furniture remover's job first since, as he was going to ride his bike there, the wind would be at the back of him. If he'd gone to the gasworks he'd have had it in his face. I didn't see the logic of it until he explained that it's not so bad having the wind in your face if you've got the job – you've got something to feel elated about. We've always done the same since then whenever we go to a pub. When it's a howling gale, we always choose a pub that the wind will blow us to – after we've had a few, we don't mind battling against it on the way back! Albert's got a lot more sense than you'd credit him for.

You'll have gathered he got the job at this furniture remover's, on a month's trial, and he was still on a month's trial when he retired twenty-two years later. Albert started at a wage of £4 4s 0d a week. It wasn't a lot of money, but our rent was low. I had ideas of not going out to work now that he was back home, but money got a bit tight, with my second son joining his brother at the grammar school. I got a grant, but the uniform cost a small fortune – it was 13s 6d just for a school cap, and they both kicked them round the playground like footballs. It used to break my heart.

Mind you, people like us, with a very low income, were

often better off than those who earned what was called a fair wage, because they came just above the grant limit: by the time they'd paid for their children's schooling, they were worse off than we were. So I decided that I'd better keep on going out to work.

I'd always avoided working in a hotel or boarding house because it seemed to me a stereotyped sort of job. There's none of the opulence and the comfort of a private house or a luxury flat, and you don't get to know the people: there's only the odd bods who stay for a while and pass on their way, to be replaced by odder bods! However, when I looked at the Situations Vacant in the local paper, nobody seemed to be looking for a treasure, but there was an advertisement for an energetic help at a Mrs Durham's Guest House. Energetic was the key word, as I discovered when I saw the place. I knew instantly that I shouldn't ring the bell, but I did.

The door was opened by this Mrs Durham, a small, birdlike woman – not the cheery sort of bird, not a robin, more like a small vulture! Her eyes were black and beady and they darted over me as she weighed me up. I must have suited her, and she must have been desperate for help anyway, because she didn't ask for any references; neither, mind you, did she trot out the usual story about her last treasure being with her for fifteen years and only leaving to look after her ageing mother, which was what most of my potential employers told me. It was their sort of reference. Later you learned that they'd had three women in as many months and the last one left in such a state of exhaustion that *she* had to be looked after by her ageing mother! Mrs Durham, I learned, had had three in four months. One left because she was too genteel and wouldn't do the steps; one had a gammy leg and could only go up the stairs one at a time, so, as the house was five storeys high, that was too time-consuming; and the last one Mrs Durham had found in bed with one of the lodgers! Although she advertised her Guest House as providing all home comforts, she felt this was stretching things a bit.

The house had seven bedrooms, two of which were permanently let, and the other five were for casuals, mostly commercial travellers. The best and the largest of the permanent rooms was let to two sisters who were both in their eighties. They'd come down in the world and were now decayed gentry. They'd been brought up in luxury, with their own personal maids to look after them, to press their clothes and brush their hair. Their parents had had a town house and a country house with a huge staff. And, like so many of their kind, the sisters retained their old aristocratic ways. They must have been absolute tartars to work for when they had the power and the glory. The elder one was supposed to be half-blind: 'Would you do this for me, Mrs Powell?' she'd say, and 'Will you get that for me, Mrs Powell? I'm not able to see well enough.' But she could see a lot better than she made out, because if ever I forgot to dust any of the many objects in the room, she'd soon tell me about it!

The other permanent boarders were two men, a chef and a waiter. They occupied the very large attic. They were what the Cockney working class called 'irons' – part of the rhyming slang 'iron hoof: poof'. Nowadays, of course, homosexual is the everyday word. I've always liked them. No matter what class they come from they seem to have an instinct for the niceties of life. They have nice manners and they understand women, somehow. They sense when you've a headache or feel a bit off colour and they're kind and sympathetic towards you. With other men who are sympathetic towards you, you feel that it's only a prelude to the old old story, so you can't get on too friendly terms with them unless you're going to be that way inclined yourself. It's one of the first rules of being a chambermaid – when you go up to make a bed, keep yourself to yourself otherwise you find that, far from making it, you're lying in it. But with my two irons I never had any of those fears. I could have all the fun of being a woman without any of the penalties!

They were very artistic, too – I've found that these sort of of men are – and they'd done all the ceiling and one wall in a delicate shade of pink, another wall was black and the rest were a sort of pale mauve. It might sound bizarre, but it was very attractive to look at. They wouldn't let me touch their room beyond making the beds, but they used to keep it absolutely spotless. I wouldn't have minded what I did for them, they were such charming and amusing people. The waiter, Charles, was inclined to be a bit more temperamental than John, the chef. That was due to the longer hours that he had to work, and the people he had to serve – perhaps having to excuse John's handiwork. John only had his kitchen staff to cope with.

They didn't have any meals in the house – they ate at the hotel – and they both worked very long hours. How they ever found energy enough to indulge in love-making, I couldn't imagine, but as they both drank heavily, that probably gave them a boost. Like all hotel workers, they got their perks. Charles used to smuggle a bottle of wine or spirits in the pocket of his tails, and John never failed to leave the kitchen without a parcel of food – which he'd often offer to me next day.

They'd been living there about six months before I came, and they seemed set for life. Then one morning as I was arriving I saw a taxi outside with luggage in, and John was leaving. When I went up and saw Charles, he was in a terrible state. Tears were streaming down his cheeks; he was flinging things about and screaming all sorts of invective about John and the waitress. This was what got Charles down. 'She won't be able to live with her – she'll find out it's only her money she's after.' Well, this she-ing and her-ing got me into a right muddle – like Shakespeare's play *Twelfth Night* or Which is Which – Viola or Sebastian. It appeared that John had been left a bit of money which had gone to his head or somewhere. Anyway, he'd changed his sex habits. I'm sure Charles wouldn't have felt nearly so affronted if it'd been another man that John was shacking up with – but to leave him for a woman! I tried to console him by saying there's as good fish in the sea and all that blarney, but he turned on me: 'You couldn't *possibly* understand,' he said, and he was right. I, a mere woman, was out of my depth, so I did the only thing possible – I left the room.

Charles went at the end of the week. Mrs Durham saw to that, and her next tenant soon altered the décor. I thought both changes were for the worse.

The liveliest boarders there were the commercial travellers

– they only stayed a night or two, but they all seemed to know each other. The evening meal used to be brightened by all their talk about the orders they'd got, the ruses they'd had to employ to get them, and the satisfied customers they'd left. After this last remark, they used to wink at each other and leave you in no doubt as to how they'd satisfied their customers!

Although Mrs Durham couldn't afford to do without the commercial travellers, she didn't really like them. She considered they lowered the tone of her 'establishment'. She called it an establishment in preference to a boarding house or guest house.

She was always talking about her family. She said she came of 'good yeoman stock'; the backbone of England. When I said that I thought the Pennine Chain was the backbone of England, she wasn't in the least amused. Neither am I, now! Mind you, if you work in a boarding house, you very soon begin to lose your sense of humour.

Mrs Durham thought that the Miss Hunts added a certain cachet to her establishment, even though they were so cantankerous and demanding. She loved the gentry, decayed or otherwise, and she had aspirations to get on a level with them. As she was at least fifty, she'd left it far too late.

My hours used to be from eight to eleven o'clock in the morning and an hour and a half in the evening to serve and wash up the dinner things. Breakfast was from eight to nine o'clock, but the old hands knew that it was wise to get down by eight as all the breakfasts were cooked at the same time, and those who came down later had anything that was going warmed up. I had to serve these breakfasts and what was going was too awful for words! Everything was bought as cheaply as possible. Even this wouldn't have been so bad if Mrs Durham had been a good cook! The scrambled eggs were little lumps of pale yellow rubber floating in some sort of liquid. It was margarine, never butter. The toast was always soggy, and when she served sausages, they were beef and, no matter how much you pricked them, they'd burst out of their skins and look most obscene. These sausages were always greeted with ribald remarks from the commercials – 'What do they remind you of, Mrs Powell?' they'd ask me. I'd keep quiet. 'No wonder they say love is blind!' I'd stifle my mirth and rush out of the room on the pretext of getting the tea. And the tea was a pretext. Talk about water bewitched and tea begrudged!

One morning, when I'd been there about two months, I answered the telephone and heard a most marvellous voice at the other end, wanting to know if there were any vacant rooms. It was one of those fascinating American voices which, compounded of dozens of accents, full of sympathy and seduction – gravelly, somehow – turn your bones to water. This one did mine – without seeing the man I could feel desire stirring in me. Ye godmothers, I must have been very susceptible in those days – I could hear gravelly voices till the cows came home now and never feel a thing! But that's what it did to me then. Even if we hadn't had a vacancy I'd have said we had, just so that he'd call and I could see him. When he did arrive, his looks belied his voice. He was either extremely ugly or homely, according to how you felt about him. But he knew the power of his voice: he sort of played on it like any virtuoso on a violin or a piano. All the boarders fell for his charm – even the men did. As for the Miss Hunts, they adored him. He called them 'ma'am', and they just loved being called 'ma'am'. He used to play cards with them, fetch their shawls and tell them funny stories – they thought he was the cat's whiskers.

It was only with Mrs Durham that his charm seemed to fall on stony ground. I thought that years of different faces and different voices had atrophied her sensibilities! Or that she was under no illusions as to the quality of her establishment and was therefore suspicious of anyone staying there for the pleasure of it. I must say that when he said he'd been recommended to the place it was a highly improbable story, as nobody in their right mind could have stayed at Mrs Durham's and looked back on it with pleasure. Perhaps he was a sociologist studying conditions in a British seaside town.

Anyway, he stayed a fortnight. It was an entertainment to see him sitting at the breakfast table, with his homely face, and to have him suddenly say in that lovely soft voice, 'This breakfast stinks!' Or, when Mrs Durham left the room after delivering some homily: 'Horse shit.' The whole table would be convulsed with laughter, everyone just warmed towards him.

It was sad the morning he left, sad and almost tragic. His cab arrived and he came down the stairs with a case in one hand and a large bunch of red roses in the other. He said his good-byes and then turned to Mrs Durham, handed her the roses and kissed her. She was speechless. I saw the tears rush to her eyes. She went straight to her room and locked the door.

When I went back in the evening, all the boarders were in a sort of a tizzy, particularly the Miss Hunts, because Mrs Durham hadn't come out of her room since the American had left. They thought she might have done herself in. Anyway, they said I was the best person to do something about it.

I knocked and knocked on her bedroom door, and at last she opened it. She was absolutely blind drunk! The room reeked of gin and her open wardrobe was full of empty bottles! I tried to get her into bed, but while I was doing this she saw the Miss Hunts peering round the door. She gave them her vulture look and then waded into them. 'Bitches!' she screamed. 'Bitches! you can take that look off your precious faces. I know who you are – bastard daughters of one of the Bloodsuckers of the Poor living on conscience money in my bloody establishment! It was your kind that sent my poor father to an early grave!' And so it went on, with her ending up by saying what she'd like to do to them if she was a man. It was a magnificent speech, I wouldn't have missed it for the world!

When the Miss Hunts went fluttering up to their room, tut-tutting all the way, she turned on the rest of us and went all maudlin. 'I'm sorry,' she said, 'I'm drunk, and I'll tell you why I'm drunk. I'm no sleeping beauty but I was treated as one this morning. He didn't mean it, of course, but I want to go on pretending he did for as long as I can.' She broke our spell by giving us a bit of invective and then disappeared into her room again. That was the only time I liked Mrs Durham.

5

IT was now that life became rather grim. I'd had a gastric ulcer. I've never mentioned my health before and I won't go on about it now. Actually, this gastric ulcer originated during the early part of the war, in London during the air raids. I believe it was because I could never give way to expressions of fear because of the children, and it was bottling up my emotions that started the ulcer off. Doctors may say this is all wrong, but that's what I think, anyway.

I'd had a bad attack eighteen months before, but now I had to go into hospital for six weeks. Poor old Albert. I reckon he had the roughest time, having to look after the home, the boys, and visit me in hospital. Then again, he hadn't been long at his job with the removal firm, and they weren't a bit pleased or sympathetic; he couldn't be sent on a big removal job since this would have meant that he'd have had to stay a night away from home, which he couldn't because of the children.

When I left hospital I still wasn't fit enough to work, and though Albert's wages had risen to £5 a week, even with the education grants for the boys there still wasn't enough to provide all the things they needed. It even grieves me now when I think of it, that my sons couldn't be the same as the other boys. And although friends and neighbours said that they should be satisfied with getting a good education and that eventually they'd earn enough money to buy all that they wanted, I didn't agree with them, because it was *then* that they wanted certain things, while they were among children who had them. To be able to buy football and cricket gear when they were grown up wouldn't compensate them at the time for the fact they couldn't have them then, when they were mixing with boys to whom their possession was in the natural course of things. You don't have to be a psychiatrist to know that nearly all children want to be the same as the others they are with, and in particular want to look the same. None of my sons has ever cared for sport and I can't help feeling that it was because they were deprived of the proper clothes and equipment.

Some people said that I was a fool to go out charring, particularly when my health wasn't too good, just to keep the boys at grammar school. Others who knew me well thought it was my own bitterness of spirit at not having been able to have a good education that drove me to make sure that they did. There were some who even hinted that I was looking on it as a kind of insurance for when Albert and I were old. Footling nonsense. I did it because I wanted to do it.

As for bitterness of spirit, if I had been bitter it would perhaps have given me more drive and ambition, and I would have done something about it. There are many people who were born in even poorer circumstances than mine, who, by dint of application and hard work, got on, so if anything I feel it was my fault that I didn't.

Albert didn't mind about our boys one way or the other. During this somewhat grim time he seemed the only contented person, which of course infuriated me. Looking back on it, I see he was right. Anyway, he didn't get ulcers. Also he was a very busy man because as well as his removal job, which was very hard work, he was doing a lot in the house, like knocking an old brick copper out of the kitchen, bits of cementing here and there, and generally getting the place into a good state of repair.

It was the beginning of this do-it-yourself game which has now become a sort of business. I remember buying Albert a magazine which showed how to make a sink unit – or that was what it was supposed to show, but as he said, you needed to be a plumber, a carpenter and a bricklayer combined. He found that out after he'd begun to dismantle the old one and then had the job of putting it together again. I didn't buy him any more magazines after that.

I think that part of my depression, and this makes me out to be very selfish, was because the boys were at grammar school. They were absorbing so much knowledge, and talking about things that were beyond my comprehension. It *galled* me, this did. It riled me that I couldn't keep up with them. Yet this, in its way, was fortunate because it made me start going to evening classes again. I'd been before to learn to make things with my hands – lampshades, gloves, upholstery and that sort of thing, but now I decided to go to classes where I had to use my brains.

I felt a bit guilty going out on what was an unproductive job, but I salved my conscience by thinking that I might become a less irritated mother and a more intelligent wife. It worked in one way, at any rate, because with increased mental alertness came far better health. I discovered that these two went together. They don't for a genius, someone like Elizabeth Barrett Browning; it was marriage that helped her. But I was no genius – for me a *'mens sana'* meant *'in corpore sano'*, and being able to write that must mean that I've learned something!

So, after poodle-faking for four months, I was able to start work again.

I got two jobs more or less at the same time, one in a flat where I went only once a week, and the other in a house where I went for three mornings.

It was a strange coincidence that both ladies I worked for were very religious – perhaps I should say both of them had a very strong faith. One lived *by* it and the other lived *for* it. The difference being that if you live *by* your faith, you don't talk about it, you just behave according to it, whereas if you're living *for* your religion, it impinges on everything you do or say.

Mrs Irving was the one who lived *by* religion. She was a Christian Scientist, and was goodness and kindness personified – more so than anyone I've ever met. For instance – and I hadn't been working for her for very long when this happened – one day I felt too ill to go to work, and Albert telephoned her to say that I wouldn't be in. As a rule, when you're going 'daily' and you get someone to ring up and say you don't feel well enough to go in, your employer says 'Oh how inconvenient, and today of all days!' – it's always 'today of all days' – and 'When will she be coming then?' and that's that. You seldom get even an expression of sympathy, but Mrs Irving said, 'Oh, I'm sorry to hear that. It'll be quite all right. Tell her not to come in until she's perfectly fit.' But that wasn't all

– that very same afternoon, she came up to see me with a pile of magazines, half a dozen eggs and a pot of cream. She made a fuss of me and repeated that on *no* account was I to come back until I was well, and then paid me my wages in advance – most of the others never paid me at all if I wasn't there! So when I say she lived by her faith, I really think that shows what I mean.

When I realized how very good a person she was, I thought that perhaps I could find something in Christian Science. I went to one of the Christian Science reading rooms a few times and then to one of their meetings. But it hadn't any message for me. I think this was because I had been brought up a Protestant, at school and Sunday school anyway, and while the Protestant clergy are not expected to be celibate, nevertheless you are made to feel that sex, even in marriage, is not meant to be enjoyable, particularly to women; it's just meant for the procreation of children. So I found it hard to accept the founder of the Christian Scientists, Mrs Baker-Eddy, who I discovered had been married three times.

Again, these Scientists believe that all illness and pain is error and needs a spiritual doctor not a physical one, as you might say. And since, during this time, I'd been suffering for weeks from an excruciating pain in my elbow, I just couldn't convince myself that it was an error! So I went to what I call a proper doctor. Mind you, if you call the Spanish Inquisition spiritual cleansing, that was the treatment I got. I thought I had rheumatism, but it turned out to be a collapsed disc, so I had to have my neck stretched. A sort of harness was put round my neck. This was attached to a long rope which was slung over a beam, then weights were put onto the end of this rope. Each time I went the weights increased. The last time there was such a heavy weight put on that I thought they were hanging me!

There was a young girl next to me having her spine stretched. She was lying on a bed which was gradually extended by being wound up, and it made a sort of creaking sound – just like the rack. Every minute I expected to hear her call out, 'I recant!'

The other job I had was with a Mr and Mrs White, and this

was a very different kettle of fish. He was what people call a rough diamond – he certainly had no polish. On the other hand he could never have been a girl's best friend, which I was told diamonds were, though I never had the opportunity of proving it. While he didn't believe in anything except himself, Mrs White belonged to an evangelical sect, similar to the Plymouth Brethren but not as strict. Mind you, people carp about evangelists: I know they're always on about the awful fate that awaits you if you stray around a bit, and they believe in hellfire, brimstone and sulphur, but nevertheless I do respect them for not pretending that the path to heaven is an easy one. I get so sick to death of these with-it clergymen with their gimmicks and pop groups, who think that adapting religion to present-day life makes everything easy. It doesn't. If you really believe in God and heaven, it's a damned hard path. I've tried it. But the more I tried and concentrated on it, the more convinced I became that it wasn't true, and as I didn't want to believe that it wasn't true, I gave up. I preferred to be as I was, an agnostic. But don't give me this 'easy way' stuff. Don't alter the Bible and the prayer books and make them easy to read. Let's keep some sort of mysticism in this prosaic world. I'd rather have fire and brimstone than pop religion and with-it clergymen.

As I've said, Mr White didn't believe in anything. He'd made his money in trade and he was sticking to it. He was a blunt-spoken man given to long diatribes about how everyone was after his money, how he'd earned it by the sweat of his brow and how none of his sponging relatives would ever get anything off him! Any relative would have had to be in desperate straits to approach Mr White for help! When he was in a good humour he was caustic and sarcastic – in a bad one he was unapproachable.

His favourite authors were Arnold Bennett and H. G. Wells, because they wrote about 'the common clay'. Mr White was always on about the fact that he came from 'common clay' and it was on the tip of my tongue to say, 'Yes, and not very well moulded either!'

Mrs White didn't let his behaviour worry her. She adopted an attitude of passive resistance, and was impervious to his sarcastic remarks about the church. She would reply, 'Yes, dear' and 'No, dear' with an air of patient resignation. If she'd been my wife I'd have gone right round the bend; with me it's not true that a soft answer turneth away wrath – it makes me even more livid!

I'd worked there about a year before adventure came to Mrs White, in the shape of Johnny and Bobby. These two were both a sort of poor man's Billy Graham. When Billy Graham comes over here he charters a plane, arrives with an army of supporters and helpers and stays in the best hotels. This Johnny and Bobby, they came over by ship – probably steerage – and were lodged by members of the faithful.

They were both in their late twenties, and although they weren't related they were similar in appearance, though this similarity wasn't so much physical as mental. Years of working together had trained them to speak and move as one man. I was reminded of one of those song-and-dance music hall acts, when every gesture, facial expression and movement is the same.

From the start I was prejudiced against them because of their little-boy names. I hate the 'Billy' in Billy Graham, but 'Johnny' and 'Bobby' are even worse. Then they seemed to make a profession of exuding boyish charm, with their smooth, bright, clean, boyish faces on which life had made no impression; not a line marred their blank surfaces, and their minds seemed as unblemished as their faces. It was as though they were impervious to the sordid and the ugly with their hygienic, disinfected minds, to which no germs of discordant ideas were able to penetrate. As far as they were concerned, there was no other path to heaven but the one they trod. And that kind of conceited complacency sends me up the wall! And another thing that riled me about them was when they told me that, in their opinion, I ranked as an equal, 'for,' they said, 'in the sight of heaven and God we're all equal, aren't we?' But as it wasn't God's domain that I was working in, I couldn't see that this was much help to me, especially as most of my employers had very different ideas on equality. The way they interpreted the Bible was that we are only equal when we're dead, and I was prepared to go along with that so long as they paid me my wages.

I began to dislike going there in the mornings to be greeted by this Johnny and Bobby, who would say in perfect unison, 'Good morning, Mrs Powell. How are we this morning?' I preferred the grunt I got from Mr White! I don't like being asked how I am first thing in the morning, and I wouldn't have told them because they'd immediately have turned on the concern and the consolation which were their stock-in-trade. They were professional dispensers of good will and though dispensing good will to me first thing in the morning is like selling refrigerators to Eskimos, such was their tenacity that they would have tried. And if I had handed out a rebuff, it would only have recharged their batteries with the milk of human kindness. Yet their happiness didn't really give pleasure, except to Mrs White. It didn't give pleasure to me and it most certainly didn't give pleasure to Mr White, or to Mrs White's friends.

Again, Mrs White's own church began to view with increasing alarm her attachment to Bobby and Johnny. The leader of her Group or Sect kept coming round to see her and it was evident that there was a rift in the evangelical lute. It was strange, because you'd have thought they were all on the same side. Instead it developed into a sort of tug-of-war for Mrs White's soul.

I suppose it was jealousy, because these evangelical sects are very small. They've got no paraphernalia, no beautiful buildings, stained glass windows, rituals and such-like. It's their members that make their church – so take one away, even though they're led on another Path to Heaven, and it's like losing a bit of the building, or at any rate a bit of the furniture.

It became increasingly evident that this spiritual to-ing and fro-ing hadn't escaped Mr White's notice. His expression, which was always craggy, became glacier-like and, far from Bobby and Johnny adding sweetness and light to the home, they were building up to the most almighty explosion. I only hoped that their stay would end and thus prevent it. The Path to Heaven that Mrs White had previously followed was at least one that didn't keep cutting across other people's way of life, but now she was exhorting all and sundry to change their ways and Be Saved before it was Too Late. Even I was subjected to a barrage of verbal persuasion as to how much happier I would be if I made an account of myself to God. When I said that I was having enough trouble settling my earthly accounts to think about heavenly ones, she reacted as if I'd struck her.

I don't think she adopted the same tactics with Mr White because, obsessed as she was, there was a limit beyond which she daren't go. Even Johnny and Bobby, encased in the armour of righteousness as they were, must have known that Mr White detested them, but in reply to all his rudeness – and they got plenty – they gave smile upon smile.

It was two days before Johnny and Bobby were leaving that they pushed their luck too far with Mr White. It was lunchtime and we were sitting round the table – I was there too because I ate with them. I sat at the end near the kitchen because I had to keep bobbing up and down serving the meal, which I'd also cooked that day because Mrs White had been to the hospital. She went there once a week, dispensing tea and sympathy to the outpatients.

I had brought in the soup and was serving it from the sideboard. 'Oh, how glad I am to see that, Margaret,' she said. 'It was freezing in Outpatients this morning.' Then she put on the bright smile which she had copied from Johnny and Bobby, and said, 'Never mind, the Lord will account it to me for righteousness.' Johnny replied, with a coy roguish look on his face, 'All our righteousnesses are as polluted garments in the sight of the Lord – Isaiah, Chapter 64, verse 6.' 'But', smiled Mrs White, 'surely righteousness exalteth a nation – Proverbs 14, verse 34.' Then up piped Bobby, 'You speak from Pride – remember, Pride goeth before destruction and a haughty spirit before a fall – Proverbs 16, verse 18.' Well, of course, you'll know that this wasn't the exact exchange of quotations, my memory's not that good, but that's the way it went, and while it was taking place, I glanced at Mr White. His face was contorted with rage. Then it happened.

'You miserable bible-thumpers!' he shouted, 'I'll give you bloody Pride and a fall with it!' He got to his feet, picked up the table and shot it and its contents over the two of them. They went back on to the floor in their chairs. 'That'll look after your effing Pride,' he said, 'and this will pollute your garments,' and he picked up the soup tureen off the sideboard and sloshed it all over them. Talk about a holocaust! Mrs White started to scream and kept it up. Johnny and Bobby were blubbing and clutching at their steaming clothes. They must have been well and truly scalded. They scrambled to their feet and rushed out of the room with Mr White on their heels: 'I'll give you five minutes to get out of the house, you praying mantises!' he shouted. I remember thinking what an apt term it was. Then he went into his bedroom and slammed the door.

Well, I didn't know whether to laugh, cry or whatever. I decided to make myself scarce and was out of the place before Johnny and Bobby.

I was left on the horns of a dilemma. What was I to do the next day? I hadn't had my wages but I don't think it was only that that made me go back. I just had to know what the outcome had been.

I arrived at the usual time. Mr White answered the door – and it was a very changed Mr White from the one I'd seen yesterday, or indeed ever before. He looked tired and dispirited: his voice and his manner were sort of softened. 'I was hoping you'd come, Mrs Powell,' he said, 'I know I ought to apologize for the way I behaved yesterday, but I can't. I had to do it, and I'm glad I've done it. I'm on my own now, Mrs White left too; perhaps she'll come back but somehow I don't think she will. I'm not sure I even want her to! I'm grateful for what you've done for us. I'd like you to stay on but I think it best all round if I make a clean break. So I'm afraid it's good-bye.' I was astonished at him. He'd never spoken more than a few words at a time before in my hearing. He held out his hand and gave me a five-pound note! I just gawped. I was speechless!

It was a pathetic ending to what had been a sad job from the start. I was the only one to come out of it with any advantage – by this, of course, I mean the five-pound note. Who would have thought that that pink-faced pair Johnny and Bobby could have caused so much drama in so short a time; and what for? To them, Mrs White could only have been another notch on their spear of righteousness, another tick in their tally of souls. I soon found a job to replace the Whites, but I kept on working for Mrs Irving for another two years.

During all this time her health began to go. I think it was because she was always doing so much to help other people that this happened. When she became very ill and was obviously in a lot of pain, I kept on at her to call a doctor, what I call a *real* doctor – she had some Christian Scientist friend praying with her – but she wouldn't. She used to say to me, 'Margaret, if I was to call in a doctor I would, in effect, be saying that something I've believed in all my life is not true.' Who could say she was wrong in her decision? Right to the end she always had a smile and a cheerful word. Shortly after she died I had a letter from a solicitor saying that in her will was written, 'I leave £10 to Mrs Powell, my treasure.' I can't say any more about her. She was too nice to talk about.

6

IF, as I do, you live in Hove, which is so much on top of Brighton that it's impossible to say where one ends and the other begins, when you are asked where you come from you say Brighton because it's a more familiar place name. People then smile or smirk. They sort of think that the place has sexual connotations. All right, Brighton got a reputation for sexual licence during the time when George IV lived at the Pavilion. But that was a few years ago and I don't believe that now it's a more frivolous town than any other seaside resort. Maybe at one time, because it was near London, men used to bring their lady friends down for the weekend. There were and are some very convenient and comfortable hotels, and they were very discreet about it. Today, when it has become London-by-the-Sea, it's far too chancy. You're almost certain to run into someone you know. Still, perhaps with the permissive society of today, that doesn't matter.

To the ordinary resident who goes into town on a weekend

to have a few pints in West Street or round the Old Steine, there never seems to be any sign of depravity. Then again, people talk about the love nests there are down there – whatever that's supposed to mean. I'll agree some funny things went on at some of the places I went to for my daily jobs, but whether you'd call them love nests or not, I don't know. Anyway, they're not restricted to Brighton, there's love nests everywhere, and if you want a dirty weekend you can have one wherever you like – in your own home, come to that.

It was round about the time that I working for Mrs Irving, in 1948, that Mae West came to Brighton. She was part author of a play, *Ladies Please*, which was being tried out at the Theatre Royal, and all the newspapers smirked about it – 'Sex Symbol Chooses Brighton for First Night'. Oh, the fun that went on! If the Prince Regent had risen from the dead, he wouldn't have had the notice taken of him that she did.

It's funny how sex symbols change over the years, isn't it? I remember a few, like Tallulah Bankhead, Pola Negri, Jean Harlow, Mae West, Greta Garbo, Marlene Dietrich, Marilyn Monroe and Raquel Welch; and when you think about them, none of them have very much in common – so nothing seems to stay the same very long, does it?

Albert and I went along and saw the play. Mae West wasn't in it, she'd written it and sat in the stalls. I don't think Albert saw anything of what went on, on the stage – he just sat with his eyes glued on Mae West. He didn't miss anything, though. The play was very poor.

I remember afterwards feeling guilty about spending the money on such a footling evening, particularly as at this time we had what was known as a Silver Lining Week, a week in which everyone exhorted everyone else on the virtues of saving money. It was really of no interest to me, as money was almost non-existent in our house, but I remember feeling almost unpatriotic that we'd spent a few bob on going to see Mae West's play.

What a lot of drivel was talked during that week! I remember the Mayor saying that our savings would go to protect our homes, our loved ones and our way of life. But as Albert was doing his best in his spare-time to stop our house from falling down, and I was looking after my loved ones, that only left the protection of our way of life, and as I was hoping for some miracle to happen to change that, his words fell on stony ground as far as I was concerned.

About this time, too, came the first whisperings of the Sussex University. One of the arguments in favour of it was that it would make Brighton an intellectual centre rather than a trippers' paradise, and it's remarks like that which infuriate me. Nobody is more for learning and education than I am, but the social implications in that statement send me up the wall. As though learning is only for a special type of person – and an educated person is necessarily a better person to have around than one who's not. I'm glad to say that Sussex University in reality is nothing like what I was given to anticipate, and that we still get visitors who come down to relax and enjoy life without bothering to be intellectual.

At this time, once again I needed some more work, so I began searching through the advertisements and came across a great rarity – a job where there was only one man to work for. Believe me, those gems very seldom came on the market, the vacancies were usually filled by word of mouth.

The advertisement read: 'Woman wanted, three to four afternoons a week for single gentleman'. Then it gave a box number, which was fortunate for him, otherwise he'd have been deluged by females – I know I'd have been round there like a shot. You may wonder at my carrying on like this and being almost disloyal to my sex, but when you work for a man it's a piece of cake. Women know how everything ought to be done, and if you don't do it their way they find out and they jolly soon tell you about it. They can't help being bossy. But if you work for a man, he leaves you alone – well, work-wise, anyway. And then, not knowing what the man was like, my imagination ran riot. I could visualize a handsome Romeo who might take a fancy to me – in a nice way, of course, and perhaps take me out occasionally, also in a nice way, of course.

These dreams never materialized, but it was good to think about them. Mind you, Albert wasn't greatly thrilled about me going after a job where there was only one man. Not that he had any worries about me being seduced or anything like that.

Very few men think that anybody else is going to fancy their wives, unless they happen to look like one of the sex symbols I mentioned earlier. No, it was for a more selfish reason. They think that if you're with another man every day, you may come back home and compare him with your husband, to your husband's detriment, and that might mean his having to change his ways. Men don't like changing their ways.

I promptly wrote after this job, but when I'd posted the letter I began to feel that I hadn't set out my qualifications well enough; for instance, I hadn't said that I used to be a cook or mentioned about my time in service. All I'd written was that I'd been doing 'daily' work, that I was used to it and could come in the afternoons, then mentioned my age and knocked a few years off it. So I sat down and wrote again, enclosing a note saying, 'Ignore previous application'. He must have thought it was funny because both letters must have come to him by the same post. Whether that's why I got the job or not I don't know.

I got a letter almost by return from a Mr Hardmore asking me to go and see him. The more I thought about the job the more I liked it. Going in the afternoons would really suit me, because it would mean that I was able to do my own work in the morning while I had plenty of energy and go to him when I'd tired a bit, instead of the other way round, which was what I'd been doing for years.

When the day came for me to go and see him, I took some time getting ready. I hadn't many things to choose from but when I'd finished I was what I would describe as respectably dressed. When Mr Hardmore answered the door, my dreams of a Romeo were immediately dashed. He was a middle-aged, rather portly man with no pretentions to good looks. But he endeared himself to me from the very beginning. He said, 'You're the only applicant I've written to', not 'I've got a number of others to see', as most people did, even though often you knew you were the only one who had applied. I've always disliked the feeling that I was being weighed in the balance – sort of 'Yes, you're *all right*, but perhaps some of the other applicants may be better'. He was a gentleman – or rather he spoke in a high-falutin' voice and anybody that spoke like that, when I was younger, I thought of as a gentleman. Bitter experience may later prove that they're not, but with me, at the beginning of any relationship, hope always abounds!

I thought he was about forty-five, and I wasn't far out, because I later discovered he was forty-nine. As I've said, he was rather fat – that was because he drank a lot, another thing I discovered later. He said, 'I'm glad you're able to come afternoons because I don't get up until about midday and I don't want anyone around then.' The wages were all right, about four shillings an hour.

He had a sort of maisonette – a basement and a first floor. Although they were big rooms, he had very little stuff cluttering up the place. I could see there wasn't going to be all that much work, and he had all the right things – hoovers and suchlike. He did his own cooking, he said, but there'd be washing-up for me to do in the afternoons. He didn't say very much at all. I could feel it was going to suit me. It did; mind you, it was a long time before I found anything out about him. I very seldom saw him. His whole waking life seemed to be spent in pubs and clubs. When the pubs shut at two or half-past, he went on to clubs until about four or five, and by that time I'd gone.

For months all we did was to write to each other – if he wanted anything in particular, he'd leave me a note, and if I wanted him to get anything in the way of household equipment, I'd leave him one. I would always start 'Dear Mr Hardmore'. He either didn't start with anything or put just 'Mrs Powell'. Some Romeo!

One day, after I'd been there several months, he came back a little bit earlier than usual and, because he was in drink, he started to chat me up. He told me that when he was in his final year at university he was left a lot of money. So much that, although he couldn't touch the capital, he could live well and easily on the interest. In a way this money ruined him, because he gave up studying and never bothered to work after that. When I asked him why, he said, 'What's the point of working when you've got more than enough to live on?'

Shortly after that I found out that he had a permanent woman friend, a Mrs Willow – a misnomer because she was

71

short and on the plump side. She was a widow.

Despite his money, I wondered why she went around with him. I could never have fancied him. He always looked messy. I suppose it was the drinking and his slack way of living. He took no trouble with his appearance. He'd gone flabby both physically and mentally.

Eventually his Mrs Willow and I got quite friendly. From what she said I gathered that she hoped to get Mr Hardmore to the point of marriage. She'd been a widow for ten years, and although she'd got two grown-up children, a son in America and a daughter married to an accountant, they wouldn't have anything to do with her. They didn't like the gay life she led going around with men and drinking. She told me she did it because she was lonely, and I could understand that. She was particularly upset about her daughter's attitude. She told me she'd twice attempted suicide because of it. I suppose it was true, but it was hard to imagine when I knew her, because, like Mr Hardmore, drink had robbed her of any real emotional feelings.

Her husband, it appeared, had been bone idle, but she said he was a great *charmer*, as though there was some special qualifications attached to being a great charmer. 'But,' she said, 'he was never unfaithful to *me* – I was his whole *life*!' I'd heard that before and found it very difficult to swallow, as I did now. After all, what's the point of being a great charmer if you don't put it to some practical use? Still, I may have been wrong. In those days it wasn't common for either a husband or a wife to deviate from the straight and narrow. They had each other and that was it. Sex wasn't the be-all and end-all of existence. Now, it seems to me, when people are thinking of getting married or, as they call it, shacking-up together, they don't consider each other in terms of integrity and honesty, the ability to work and their qualities as parents. It's 'is he or she any good in bed?' My godfathers! I know you spend a third of your life, that's eight hours a day, in bed, but out of that eight hours surely only a very small portion can be devoted to love-making? If I'm being old-fashioned, all I can say is that there's a different race of men knocking around now than when I was young!

72

I don't deny that sex in marriage is important but it isn't the be-all and end-all and it isn't that difficult. It's like many other things – the more you think about it the more worried you get. I mean, despite the *Kama Sutra* and the goodness knows how many ways of making love it contains, essentially they're all more or less the same. My contribution to sex education is: don't worry about it too much.

As I say, Mrs Willow was convinced that her husband had never been unfaithful to her, and she went on about it. As if I cared one way or another! Apparently he used to call her pet names like 'baby-love', 'my violet' and 'little flower'. Now if I'd been her I'd have kept that to myself. It's funny, isn't it, how people who are given these sort of names don't realize that years have passed since they looked like a little flower or a violet. They were given them because of their charming manner or babyish ways. But at any rate, in Mrs Willow's case, passing years and buckets of gin had taken their toll of her sweetness and innocence.

She told me she was looking for a similar type to him and from the way in which Mr Hardmore's name kept cropping up, it was obvious the direction in which she was looking. But she could have saved herself the trouble. Mr Hardmore was married to the bottle.

I wasn't sorry that he showed no disposition to marry her. Although I quite liked her, it wouldn't have been the same working for him and her. I much preferred him single. As I've said, that way the job suited me.

Although now Mr Hardmore and I began to meet more often, we still regularly passed our little notes. There was one day when he bought an antique bed. It was a huge thing, almost as wide as it was long. He left me a note about it: 'Mrs Powell, Would you please get a tin of furniture polish and see what you can do on it.' The following day I left one back. 'Dear Mr Hardmore, I've polished your bed but there's not much I can do on it on my own.' But he never took it up. I couldn't make first base with him. I wasn't trying to get fresh with him, it was just that I wanted to be noticed. I suppose, in a way, that I needed to test my power of attraction and though I would have fought to the last ditch for my virtue, I wanted it in a way to be challenged. It's the excitement of the chase, isn't it? It's not the *getting* – you don't really *want* what you get. When I think of the various young men I got, and when I'd examined the prey, the trouble I had getting rid of them! I never had the courage to tell them point blank that I'd changed my mind and gone off them; that they weren't what I thought they were or what I was really looking for. I'd write them notes the same as I did with Mr Hardmore, saying, 'I don't think we're really suited to each other, so I don't want to waste your time. This is just to say good-bye.' Don't take me too literally – I didn't write them to Mr Hardmore. Nor, as you must have gathered, did I really think about him in that way. He was just a challenge.

He was also a very eccentric man. I don't know if you've noticed, but when rich men are peculiar, it's called eccentricity. But when poor people act a bit strange, they're promptly classed as loony!

After I'd been at Mr Hardmore's some time, he and a few of his cronies formed a sort of dining club. They used to meet once a month at his flat, and I did the cooking for them. Apart from the joy of choosing and cooking good food again, it was also well paid. The guests were very generous, both in their compliments and their tips.

They always had a couple of show girls down from London at these affairs, and according to Mrs Willow they'd do a sort of strip-tease show later in the evening. She was most disparaging about them. I remember her saying, 'If I took as long to remove my clothes as those girls do, it wouldn't be worth going to bed with him – he'd have passed out before I got in!'

Every job has its perks, and this one was no exception. Mr Hardmore said to me quite early on, 'Always help yourself to any drink you fancy when you fancy it, Mrs Powell.' Well, it was some time before I took him at his word. I'd always thought that drinking alone was sort of sinful, but I was able to salve my conscience by saying to myself that the more I drank the less there'd be for Mr Hardmore, and since he was an alcoholic, I was doing him a good turn.

It didn't do any good, of course. By now his whole life was

spent drinking and where there's an endless supply of money there's an endless supply of drink. Occasionally he would try and pull himself together and go away to one of these homes where he got sort of dehydrated. I would still keep going in to dust the flat, and he'd come back looking a different man, with bright eyes and colour in his cheeks. But it never lasted. He very soon slipped back into the old ways. He got so that he blamed his condition on money. 'Money is an evil thing,' he told me, 'that's why I spend it on evil things and in an evil way.' When I said that if he wanted to, he could do good with his money, he said, 'No, if I give my money to help people they will grow to rely on it as I have. All money that isn't earned by the sweat of one's brow is evil.' You see what I mean about him being eccentric. I suppose in fact he was only trying to look for a philosophy to justify his behaviour.

I did the same over helping myself to his drink. Because, acting on the assumption that it would be the only job I'd ever have in which there was free drink, I persevered at my task. I'd go home in the evening and breathe alcohol fumes all over Albert, which drove him into a fury. Not that he minded my drinking, but he'd say, 'Why don't you bring some home?' 'No,' I'd say, 'that would be stealing.' That helped my conscience.

I worked there for seven years. Then the inevitable happened. Mr Hardmore died of cirrhosis of the liver; he was only fifty-six. It seemed a terrible waste of a man. He hadn't made a will, but as he couldn't touch his capital there wasn't much he could leave. Mrs Willow was expecting £500, which he'd promised her. And he probably did mean her to have it, but I suppose like many people, he hadn't made a will because of the superstition that it hastens death.

Mrs Willow had told me that he was going to leave me £50. I wasn't disappointed. During my years in service I had met so many old servants who had been persuaded to stay with their employers because they would be mentioned in their wills, and on their deaths had got nothing, that it was like water off a duck's back to me.

I went to the funeral with Mrs Willow, and a lot of publicans and sinners! It was my first experience of a cremation. I was amazed at the speed we rushed through the streets. You'd have thought a gang of body-snatchers were after us and we wouldn't get there with the coffin intact! We went up a long gravelled path to the crematorium and I could see the chimney belching out smoke which I thought was of the body of the funeral before ours. As we were leaving, up came another funeral party. Talk about death on a conveyor belt! There were none of the trimmings and paraphernalia of death that I'd remembered. Mind you, I hadn't been to a funeral for years; at the last one there had been horse-drawn carriages, widow's weeds, the lot.

I remember going to one as a child. My sister and I were given new black dresses of thick serge bound with black braid – we even had black-edged handkerchiefs in which to shed the appropriate tears for the 'dear departed'. The men all had dark suits, black ties and bowler hats. I particularly recall that after the burial service we were all standing round the graveside and the clergyman was giving us a few homilies for good measure. 'Mourn not too deeply, my friends,' he said, 'we will all meet again in Heaven,' and the woman next to me muttered, 'Not if I have my way we won't!' It made me want to laugh so much that I had to pretend to be crying.

From the graveside we all went back to the funeral feast, and a feast it was for us children. There were chickens, cooked meats, salads, jellies and trifles and fruit, and we all sat down at table. I remember that, at first, everyone was very solemn and spoke in measured, grave tones or whispers, about the 'dear departed', particularly someone whom we used to call Uncle Fred, though he wasn't really any relation of ours. He'd laid a wreath on the grave in the shape of a harp – a sort of reminder to us all that the departed would very soon be playing one!

But before long the atmosphere changed – it was after the barrel of beer had been tapped. Everybody got loud-voiced and jolly and they talked away about Jessie – that was the dear departed's name – about what a hard life she'd had with her late husband, who'd spent all his time in the pub, 'for which I don't blame him', I heard Uncle Fred mutter, what she must have suffered with her rheumatism and what a happy release it was now that she'd 'passed over' – nobody ever died then among the working class, they always 'passed over'. But for all this talk, good or bad, about the dear departed, they did, as it were, give her a sort of testimonial, didn't they? Her life meant something, if only for a day. I think people ought to go out of this world with a bit of pomp and ceremony: you come into it with precious little, it's a pity if you can't leave it with a bit more!

7

AFTER the whooping it up at Mr Hardmore's, Albert wasn't at all keen on my getting another job. In spite of the fact that I'd told him I only drank to remove temptation from my employer, Albert was unconvinced. I was glad that he was – I wouldn't have wanted a husband who was as stupid as that! By the time I'd had an afternoon's session with Mr Hardmore and Mrs Willow, I'd go home so merry that any idiot could have told that self-sacrifice was far from my thoughts.

I didn't look on Albert's attitude as an unwelcome intrusion on my liberty because I knew that he'd very soon change his mind when he discovered that there wasn't enough money for us to have a pint or two on a Saturday night. The freedom also gave me the opportunity to think about my own home.

I set to and had an absolute orgy of cleaning. Although we couldn't afford to refurbish, wallpaper and paint were comparatively cheap, so I got Albert on the job of redecorating. We'd just bought the house, so it was up to us to keep it in good order.

We'd decided to buy when the new Rent Act came in, and we found that, in one fell swoop, our rent was going up from £1 2s 6d a week to £1 16s 0d, and that was only on a three-year agreement. It was a near certainty that when the three years were up, we'd have to pay even more.

I was fairly crafty in the way I went about buying the house. This Act, although it allowed landlords to put up the rent, also stipulated that they must do essential repairs and outside painting, and although our landlady hadn't neglected her properties, she just hadn't the money to do this extra work in the terms of the new Act. I thought, therefore, that she would be glad to sell one of them, at any rate, to raise the cash to repair the others. Next time she came round to collect the rent I asked her whether she would sell it. She said she would let it go for £700. By dint of bargaining, I got her down to £675 which, although it was an old terrace house, was, nevertheless, very cheap indeed.

The council loaned us £700 – the extra £25 for a few necessary repairs – so I consider we were very fortunate indeed. Particularly as now, although the loo is still in the yard and the bath in the kitchen, we could sell it for £3,300, because that was the price paid for a similar one up the road only a week or two ago.

As I've said, I'd got Albert on to the decorating. At that time it was all the rage to have a different coloured wallpaper on one wall from the other three, so I decided to follow the fashion. But what I hadn't realized was that whereas in a modern house this new style might be all right, in our place, with rooms square like a rabbit hutch, and very little larger, it wasn't really on. When we'd finished, it looked as if we'd run out of wallpaper three-quarters of the way through and had been unable to get any to match it!

We'd done one wall in red and the other three in a white paper covered with what appeared to be red forget-me-nots. We'd also done the ceiling in a sort of pink. We felt very much with-it, though I noticed that Albert always took his glasses off now when he went to sit in there. Just after it was finished our ex-landlady came round for a chat, so I took her in to see what we'd done. She went back on her heels a bit; 'It's transformed,' she said, but by the way she said it I had a suspicion that she was glad she'd sold us the place.

I know a lot of people complain about the rapacity and the greediness of landlords, but I must say our landlady was always very fair to us. For years we'd only paid 22s 6d a week for this seven-roomed house, which included the rates, so she certainly hadn't been able to make much out of it, and yet, without any grumbling, she'd always done the repairs, and she'd never minded if we couldn't pay the rent punctually.

We'd always wanted her to put a damp-course in, but she couldn't afford it, so of course we always had rising damp in our front room – we still have. We've kept meaning to have it done but never got round to it, and this winter it's risen higher than ever before – it nearly reached the ceiling! It's like your third cup of tea – wet and warm.

As I expected, after two or three weeks of us being stony broke, Albert suggested that I might like to look for a job, a *different* sort of job this time. He felt a bit sheepish about it, but now that I'd got the house in some sort of shape I was getting bored. You might think that having a seven-roomed house and a husband and three sons to look after would have been plenty to do, but, in my own home, I've never been a fanatic about housework – so long as it's clean and tidy, and looks like a home, that's all right with me. I've never wanted my home to be a show-piece.

There are some people who, when you go into their houses, expect you to wear your shoes out rubbing them on the front mat, and next they'd like you to take them off as if it was some sort of Buddhist temple. Then when you sit down they rush at you with ash-trays in case you might drop some on the floor. And the moment you get out of your chair they plump the cushions up. What sort of a home is that? It may look lovely, but it's certainly not a joy for ever. It reminds me of my grandmother's front parlour, which was never used except on a Sunday afternoon when we all assembled there under the supervision of our parents. There my grandfather would read the Bible to us, and woe betide anyone who put his feet on the rungs of the chairs or did anything untoward.

But, to the business of getting a job, and a different sort of job – what could I do? I wasn't trained for anything outside domestic service, I didn't fancy being a shop assistant. No doubt I could have got work in a store but at that time they weren't employing people part-time. So I decided to advertise myself in our local evening paper. The advertisement read: 'Capable woman requires part-time work mornings or afternoons'.

I got some very peculiar replies. One potential employer wanted a woman who was 'not afraid of hard work'. Well, if there's anything more calculated to put you off a job than somebody telling you they want someone who's not afraid of hard work... Nothing would induce me to take a job like that. It's always going to be fairly hard work even if they don't mention it, so that if they *say* the work's hard, what they obviously want is a kind of female Samson.

Another reply was from a man who kept an antique shop. He wanted someone to do a bit of 'light dusting and then occupy herself in any way that she liked'. This appealed to me. I could visualize myself flitting round dusting a few highly valuable objects and then sitting in the shop waiting to serve customers; it seemed very inviting. But Albert didn't like the sound at all of that 'occupy' yourself – he probably thought the man wasn't nearly as antique as the things he sold in his shop. He wouldn't let me go after this one, which grieved me at the time.

One reply, which I thought might do, was for me to read the newspaper to an elderly lady whose eyesight was failing. Albert couldn't fault this one, it must be harmless. There'd be no whooping it up in a job like that. I think, in his mind's eye, he sort of envisaged me as a kind of Florence Nightingale, bringing sweetness and light to an old, frail and helpless lady. I took it, but it didn't turn out a bit like that. She wasn't in the least frail or helpless. All right, her eyesight was failing, but this had turned her sour so that her disposition was such that an angel couldn't have dispensed sweetness and light to her.

I lasted exactly one week. I did two hours a morning at five shillings an hour, reading first *The Times* newspaper and then a book. I must say, I enjoyed it hugely. Then came the terrible shock. I thought by now that I'd got rid of my inferiority complex, but what happened brought it surging back, and with interest. When I'd finished reading on the first Friday, she handed me my wages and then said, 'And here's another week's salary in lieu of notice. You see, Mrs Powell,' she went on, 'although I can't tolerate your voice any longer, I'm nevertheless extremely grateful to you. My doctors have said that I should learn Braille, but I thought that by having someone to read to me for two hours a day I could save myself the trouble. But in one week you have provided me with the greatest incentive to learn it that I could have had. I'm starting next week.' Then she went on, 'Until I've learnt Braille I shall make do with the BBC, which I've found so much more enjoyable over the last few days!' Talk about taking sweetness and light to a frail, helpless old lady!

I can laugh about it now, but I was terribly grieved at the time. I was in tears all the way home. What an embittered old so-and-so she was to take it out of me like that.

When Albert came back home that evening I tried to take it out of him. 'Why did you let me go for the job,' I said, 'when you must have known my voice was so awful?' But as I've said, it's impossible to quarrel with Albert; he just replied, 'Oh well, as well as losing her eyesight she must have defective hearing into the bargain. You ought to feel sorry for her instead of making all this fuss.' That's the best of old Albert; he's been a husband in a million to me, though I'd never let him know it. There's one good thing that came out of that job – I learnt to read and enjoy *The Times*!

Immediately after I'd left, I got a letter from the woman in the flat above asking if I'd be prepared to take her two poodles out for a walk twice a day for the same money. Not being a dog lover, I turned it down. I don't dislike dogs, it's just that I always feel so conspicuous when I'm out with one. Dogs stop at every tree or lamp-post and tug at the lead as though their very life depended on it. Dogs in the country may be all right, where there aren't all these inducements to loiter, but I'm not going to move there just to find out.

It seemed to me that I was a bit unlucky with jobs around this time because I only stayed at the next one I took for a few weeks. It was with a woman who had a family of four children, all under eight years old.

Normally I'm very fond of kids, and I've never minded working in a place where there were children, but here I found that as soon as I arrived in the morning, my employer would go out, leaving me in charge of the children. I didn't mind that at first, but what I did mind was that she expected to find all the work done when she got back. And it was such a swindle.

For the four-and-six an hour, which she was paying me, she was getting a daily and a baby-sitter as well. And those kids – godfathers! I'll never forget them if I live to be ninety! They were angelic while she was around, but as soon as she went out they became fiends out of hell. They'd fight among themselves and then gang up on me when I tried to stop them, they'd pile into the room I was clearing, play with the switches on the hoover, then pull the plug out, hide my dusters and hand-brush, use the brooms as hobby horses and plaster their faces and clothes with the floor polish. It was all too harassing!

In the end I told her about it and how rude they were. All right, she was cross with them and ticked them off, but she was never the same to me after that, because no mother – particularly one whose children are well behaved when she's around – likes to think that they're any different when she's out. They think it's you; that either you don't know how to look after them or you've got a sour disposition which makes you dislike children. In any case, the children's behaviour didn't improve, so I gave in my notice. I made the usual excuse that my mother had fallen down the stairs and broken her leg.

The number of times this has served as an excuse to leave jobs, both for me and my sister, Mother would need to be a centipede just to keep up with all her broken limbs! It's a good job she's lived so long – she's now in her ninetieth year – otherwise we'd have had to have kept on resurrecting her! We used to tell her so. We used to say to her, 'You can't die, Mum – you've got to stay alive so that we can keep on breaking your legs!' Although, of course, strictly speaking, we were lying, I think we were doing our employers a kindness by using this method, because nobody likes to think that you're fed up working for them, do they? Just as it wasn't necessary for that old cow to tell me she couldn't stand the sound of my voice.

So I got another 'daily' job. Another one that satisfied Albert, working for a Miss Ellis.

This time I struck lucky. She was a very pleasant spinster, the flat was centrally heated, labour-saving and a complete change from the somewhat Spartan surroundings of my own home, where we still couldn't afford luxuries like carpets, or too much in the way of heating. Another thing I very much appreciated was that when Miss Ellis found that we hadn't a bathroom, she let me use her bath – and not only her bath, her soap and towels too. Cor, talk about comfort and luxury ...! I absolutely revelled in it. There was a lovely chunk of scented soap, not like our carbolic, and an enormous towel that wrapped right round me, instead of a tiny one that only dried a few inches at a time. Then again there was a sense of freedom and peace, not like having a bath in the kitchen, and when anyone wants to go to the loo they have to walk through. And Albert has always been a bit coy about exposing himself so, as soon as he got out of the bath, he used to try to make himself a sort of skirt out of the towel. It was so small that he couldn't get it to go right round, so he had to cover the most important portion of himself and move himself around as the person crossed the room. As I've said to him many a time, it's all false modesty when all's said and done.

When I told them at home about this bathing privilege Miss Ellis gave me, they were very envious – particularly Albert. I think he was more jealous of the baths than the drinks I got from Mr Hardmore. Miss Ellis did once say to me that Albert could bath there too, but I didn't tell him that. I like to keep my working life quite separate from home life. Albert wouldn't have wanted me appearing at his job, saying could I have a ride in one of the furniture vans, so I didn't want him coming to mine.

Miss Ellis was about sixty years old. Her only relative was a bachelor brother who lived in Manchester. Her parents, who were both now dead, had also lived in Manchester where her father had made his money in trade. Although she had a lot of money, she hadn't had a proper education. She'd had a governess as her father didn't believe in educating girls. He thought it was the ruin of them, that it gave them ideas, and he didn't believe in women having ideas.

There are still men of the older generation today who think that education has been the ruin of women, that all they really need to know is how to get married, cook and bring up a family.

Miss Ellis told me her mother had died of some obscure complaint. Then she showed me a photograph of her father, and if ever I've seen an obscure complaint, here was the picture of one! Miss Ellis was then seventeen, and she took over the running of the house – and a hard, unrewarding job it must have been. But I haven't got all that sympathy for the women of those days. They made a tyrant of a husband or a father by never having a thought or a life of their own. They allowed a man to feel all-powerful, and although, in the home, power may not corrupt, it feeds on itself so that men eventually can't stop exercising it on any and every occasion. That's what happened with Victorian husbands and fathers, I think, and it was the women that allowed it to happen. After all, one must suppose that when husbands got married they had some deep feelings for their wives and that was the time when women could have established the pattern of their lives together. It comes back to the old cliché 'Begin as you mean to go on'. When a man is violently in love with you, when you can turn off sex for him – and, presumably, even Victorian husbands didn't actually force their wives – when you can say no to sex unless you get your way, you've got all the power in the world. It's no good, ten years after you've been married, waking up to the fact that your husband is dictatorial and you don't like it, and then trying this formula, because in those ten years you'll have lost a lot of the attraction you had for him and he'll have got set in his ways, and a man doesn't like to change except perhaps by looking elsewhere for the comforts you are denying him.

Of course, Miss Ellis wasn't in the position of denying her father anything, nor was she likely to be able to deny any man, because she showed me a photo of herself at the time and she was plainness personified. I know there weren't all the aids to good looks in those days – hairdressing and cosmetics and that kind of thing – but I felt that anyone at seventeen had a right to look better than Miss Ellis did. Mind you, having been a plain girl myself, I was able to sympathize with her.

One of Miss Ellis' disabilities was a large mole on her chin, unattractive in itself but made worse by a large, strong hair that sprouted out from the middle of it, and whenever she talked, this hair would waggle to and fro like a conductor's baton – I couldn't keep my eyes off it. When we became more friendly, I said to her, 'Why don't you have that mole removed by a surgical operation?' She could have afforded it and I thought that she just needed someone to jog her into having it done. But oh no! She told me that her mother and her grandmother had both had a similar mole on their chins – it was a sort of family heirloom and therefore she couldn't possibly have it removed. All I can say is, that if I were descended from Catherine the Great and if she'd had a mole on her chin, I'd still have *mine* taken off.

I'm a great believer in any kind of surgery that makes you look more attractive. It's absolute rubbish when people say, 'Oh yes, I know she's plain but her personality is so strong that you forget her plainness.' It didn't work out that way as far as I was concerned. I thought that I'd got an interesting person-ality when I was young, but judging by the number of young men who took me out once and never renewed the acquaint-ance, they didn't seem able to forget my plainness. Particu-larly when, as in my case, plainness was allied to virtue. I know they say that virtue is its own reward, but that's cold comfort to a young girl.

Although Miss Ellis didn't get married, at least she had money to console her. Not that she was miserable: she had her life's work, her book, to occupy her mind and knitting (for overseas missions) her hands. The things she knitted didn't conform to the pattern. She dropped as many stitches as I do aitches, but a lot of love went into the work. When I remarked that I thought most overseas missions were in countries with a very hot climate and that therefore they didn't need woollies, she told me that her things went to missions in Siberia. I found this hard to swallow. After all, I know the Russians send people to Siberia, perhaps more so then than now, but it was the first I'd heard of them allowing missionaries there! How-ever, I thought it best not to pursue the subject; I didn't want her to feel that part of her life's work was going down the drain.

Her other great work, the work of her mind, was the book she was writing: *Romantic Love through the Ages*. The way she said it, the reverential tone of voice she used, you'd have thought it was a new Bible she'd been on for years.

She used to read extracts of this book to me during our coffee break. Again, she was the democratic kind of employer. In exchange for the friendliness of sitting together, I had to listen to this awful mush. She'd begun the book at the time of what I describe as knights in armour, and worked through the ages to the twentieth century. I must say that most of her romantic lovers I'd never heard of, although I'd read many books on mythology. I suppose the advantage was that nobody could refute any of her stories. The same with those about the troubadours and serenaders. I never did care much about them, they always struck me as sort of half-queers, going around strumming beneath people's windows or singing away to the old-fashioned equivalent of a guitar. They were sort of pink-blooded people. All their love went into their music, they never had anything left for afters.

Miss Ellis was always pumping me as to my views on romantic love, especially on a Monday morning. She had the completely erroneous idea that the working-class weekend was devoted to love-making. One morning I got so exasperated that I said, 'You know, Miss Ellis, you've got a completely false impression about working-class people. Working-class people don't go in for romantic love!' So she said, 'Oh, don't they? What sort of love do they go in for?' I said, 'Their love is from sheer necessity – a merciful release from the mundane!' 'But surely,' she said, 'a lot went on below stairs? I remember when I was young and we had a big staff of servants, the butler, the footman and the gardener were always larking with the maids. An under housemaid of ours was dismissed because she was pregnant by one of them.' 'How do you know it was one of the menservants?' I said. 'It could have been your brother or one of the visitors.' She was horrified at this. She was like all the rest, she couldn't conceive of anyone of her class mixing with anyone below their station or straying off the straight and narrow with them. So I told her a thing or two I'd seen going on on the back stairs between the men of the house and the housemaids and parlourmaids. It wasn't romantic love I told her about, it was plain, straightforward 'Get up them stairs'!

I seldom saw anything going on between the men and

women servants. Which is strange when you think that we were well fed and comfortable, in warm surroundings and in close proximity – certainly the temptations were there. Our employers were contradictory in their attitude to us. They would give us exhortations on sobriety and morality yet they'd shut us up together and present us with opportunities for dalliance. I suppose they didn't think that servants could feel sexually inclined towards each other, and in a way they were right. After working a fourteen-hour day, most of us wanted bed not bed-mates!

But getting back to Miss Ellis and her romantic love. Among her favourite authors were Rhoda Broughton, Ethel M. Dell and Baroness Orczy with her *Scarlet Pimpernel* – Miss Ellis loved the Scarlet Pimpernel; all the rescues that he did, his chivalry and everything. I must say I thought I'd outgrown him with his daring feats which seemed so very far-fetched, but since having more recently read of some of the marvellous rescues that were attempted in the last war, perhaps I've done Baroness Orczy an injustice.

But although these authors were popular in their day, really their day has passed, and even in the 1950s they seemed dated. Still, to Miss Ellis, they were a pattern of the kind of love that she wanted to believe in, and there are still people today who need the same kind of assurance. Look at women's magazines with their advice to the lovelorn. It's the first thing readers turn to. They may pretend to be sending it up, but they're not. There are still many Miss Ellises at heart.

When she asked me to make any criticisms of her book, I never said what I *really* thought of it. But I don't consider that I was being a hypocrite, even when I praised it. After all, it might not have been as bad as I thought! As I've said, I was no expert on romantic love, or ordinary love for that matter. Being a char was no passport to the former and it made me too tired for the latter!

Above all the others I've mentioned, Elinor Glyn was Miss Ellis' favourite author, and, in her day, she was considered very daring. Miss Ellis really believed in that book *Three Weeks*, where the heroine, isolated at night with a handsome young man, and being so afraid that he would molest her –

although he was supposed to be a gentleman – tried to keep awake and hold him off at gun point. Eventually she fell asleep, and therefore married him because she was convinced he'd made love to her while she was asleep. Now how could anyone believe that drivel! From my experience, it's absolutely impossible for anyone to make love to you in your sleep, and as for doing it if you were a virgin, well ...! But Miss Ellis thought it all possible. Mind you, I found she wasn't averse to a detailed description of *why* it couldn't be done!

It was around this time that her brother, who lived in Manchester, came to stay. He was a very different type, nothing like as democratic as she was. He was one of the real old school, who never could, or never would, alter their conviction that, by virtue of their money and education, they were superior beings.

I could tell that he didn't like me calling him Mr Ellis, he thought that I should say 'sir'. As his sister told me, back home he had an old family retainer looking after him, who always called him 'sir', and in moments of emotion 'Master Clive'! Well, maybe the old man was happy doing this, his life had been one round of service, but I certainly wasn't going back to that way of behaving.

The whole week that he stayed in the flat Mr Ellis said no more than Good Morning to me. Miss Ellis herself seemed half-afraid of him, and no mention was made of her great book. Most of his time was spent going through her accounts and checking up on the money she'd spent. Although I was glad of a rest from *Romantic Love through the Ages*, I was also pleased to see the back of Mr Ellis.

Shortly after his visit we were discussing the current chapter, and I said, 'You know, Miss Ellis, you don't go out and do any research. You should study present-day romance by observation.' I didn't intend her to take this remark up, I just said it as something to say. 'But where can I go? All the people I know are around my own age.' So, again laughingly, I said, 'Why don't you go into a pub occasionally – you'll see people of all ages there.' Much to my surprise, she immediately came back at me, 'Oh Margaret, I'd like to do that. Will you come with me one evening? I'll pay all the expenses of course.'

Well, what could I do? I could think of better ways of spending the evening than sitting in the pub with my elderly employer, but I hadn't the heart to refuse to go with her, and a drink's a drink in any company. I knew Albert wouldn't mind, not with her. In any case, it was my own fault for getting away from the worker-employer relationship.

So, a week later, we started out. And I must admit that Miss Ellis, in spite of what I've said about her, didn't look too bad. Her clothes may have been old-fashioned but they were good quality and, though by contrast I was more up-to-date, anyone could tell at a glance who had the money.

I took her to a very lively pub in Brighton, and it was fascinating to me to see how she reacted to the noise and the people. She really thought she was seeing life in the raw, yet in fact they were just ordinary people having a normal weekend's jollification. She drank two sherries and felt she was whooping it up. Her reactions reminded me in some way of an account I'd read in the local paper about a meeting of the Lord's Day Observance Society. It was held to protest against a campaign for Brighter Sundays for Brighton, and in particular against a suggestion that there should be an extra half-hour's drinking time. One of the organizers said that Brighton would become another Babylon!

As I say, Miss Ellis drank two sherries, but, Babylonian that I am, I had three! I would have liked to have plumbed the depths of iniquity and had four, but I didn't like to sting her for any more, and she wouldn't let me pay for anything. She felt she'd had herself a ball. She couldn't stop talking about it. So I knew it wouldn't be long before she'd suggest repeating the experience. She did, and this time she really smartened herself up with new clothes, the lot. If it hadn't been for that hairy old mole, she wouldn't have been unattractive.

I took her to a different pub, and coming back from the bar with the drinks, I found her in conversation with two men. One was about thirty-five and the other a bit younger. They were Canadians – the elder, whose name was Pete, said they'd liked England so much when they were here during the war that they'd decided to come back. This may have been true, but it's my bet that they were a couple of army deserters.

I could see that Miss Ellis, or Thora, as she'd asked me to call her when we were out together – 'Call me Thora,' she said; it reminded me of that Victorian ballad 'Wait, wait, wait for me, Thora', except there was no wait about it: my Thora was striding in deep – I could see that she was absolutely captivated by these two men and their Canadian accents. I was, too, when I first heard them, but my hearing coarsened with their behaviour. Not so my Thora's, her ears were flapping as she listened to a load of hot air from this Pete. She was lapping him up like a thirsty traveller would water in the Sahara! That left me with the younger one. He wasn't too loquacious. It may be, of course, that when I informed him that I didn't want to hear about his ranch in Alberta, or how many head of cattle he had, or how he missed the old home-stead, that I didn't want to see pictures of those he'd left behind him, and, finally, that I didn't want to hear how much prettier English girls were – it may be I robbed him of his talking point!

But, as I say, Miss Ellis – or Thora – was entranced by her Pete. I didn't at that time realize how much she'd been taken in by him. When we left together at closing time she talked about him all the way back to her home: what an interesting life he'd had, what good manners he'd got – 'a proper Sir Walter Raleigh', she said, sort of pretending that it was all a part of her research on *Romantic Love through the Ages*. What I should have told her was that, from my war-time experiences, I'd found many of them to be Sir Walter Raleighs. They'd lay down their cloaks for you to step on and when you did they'd pull them from under you so that they could get you on your back as quickly as possible. Yes, I know!

But what I didn't know was that she'd given this Pete her address and invited him round to the flat. So I was very annoyed and disconcerted when, on the following morning, he called at eleven o'clock, and I had to make coffee for three instead of two. This was the start of regular visits. He felt that he'd got her where he wanted her. At first he was quite attentive to me, although he sensed that I was antagonistic towards him. But as soon as he knew, and his sort always know, that Miss Ellis had completely fallen for him, and that no warnings from me would have any effect on her, he ceased to be more than barely polite to me. When I opened the door he'd sail past me without even bothering to say Good Morning. He didn't like me having coffee with them because he knew I was sitting in judgement on everything he said, and might try and warn her off afterwards. But he captivated her so quickly that no warnings from me would have had any effect.

I knew she was giving him money. One day he came in wearing a new watch, and on another he'd a gold cigarette case. It annoyed me how a woman of her age could be so deluded. Surely she should have known that a young man of thirty-five couldn't have fallen in love with even an attractive woman of over sixty, let alone a plain one with a hairy old mole. Eventually I did try telling her that he was just after her money, but she wouldn't listen to me. 'He's like a son to me,' she kept repeating. 'A right bastard son you'll find him to be,' I flung at her in my exasperation.

I got so worried, because in a way I felt terribly responsible for it all. Albert told me to pack the job in, but I couldn't somehow. I felt I would be leaving her to her fate. I could see what the end would be and yet what could I do? There was no law against an infatuated woman giving her money away, however worthless or crooked the recipient was.

Then things got worse. This Pete moved into the flat, sleeping in the spare room, and he used the place as if it belonged to him. He now quite openly asked Miss Ellis for money even in front of me, and I could tell it wouldn't be long before he had me out of the place.

So, at last, I did something, something which I'm still not able to convince myself was the right thing. I wrote to her brother in Manchester, explaining as well as I could what was happening and yet not making Miss Ellis out to be as stupid as she was being. I didn't do it for my own sake. I knew it could never benefit me. I knew that, as soon as her brother realized that it had all started because we had gone out together, he'd be even more certain than ever that one should never mix with the lower classes.

The moment he got my letter he was down, and the same day Pete was out of the flat. How he did it I don't know. He was a retired solicitor, and they seem to have a way of doing these kind of things. But not only did he get rid of Pete, he made Miss Ellis leave Brighton and go to live with him in Manchester. He said she hadn't got enough sense to live on her own.

It was this that made me feel so awful about having written to him. I had, as it were, turned the calendar back forty years. She was again keeping house, just exchanging a martinet of a father for a martinet of a brother. And all because of me. When I said good-bye to her, she didn't reproach me. I think she felt that the moment of happiness she had had made everything worth while. She'd had her taste of what, to her at any rate, was romantic love – but I'll bet she never finished her book.

8

IT was about this time that Albert had a first-hand experience of life below stairs. I don't mean by that that he changed his job as a furniture remover, but his firm sent him to a large house in the country, and he had to pack the china, glass, pictures and the valuable ornaments, of which they had many.

He was there for three days. He slept in a small room next to the kitchen. All the servants were in residence; the chauffeur used to bring him a cup of tea in the morning and he had his meals with the servants.

Although Albert denies it now, he never really believed the tales I told him about the rigid hierarchy of the servants. I could sense he thought that my stories sort of grew in the telling; that when you're young you're impressionable and you see things in the wrong perspective. But he admitted after his stay in that mansion that I hadn't exaggerated at all. The housekeeper there had been the nanny, but since the children had married or left home, she took on the duties of housekeeper, and a proper old martinet she was. She was always talking about 'our dear Queen' – meaning Queen Victoria, of course; what an example she was to the tone of any house – apparently she set a lot of store on that word 'tone'. Albert said it was as if she'd been asleep for fifty years and had just woken up!

She had her meals served in her own room by the kitchen-maid and, as it had been in my days in service, it was called The Pug's Parlour. I don't know why, but again, it was interesting to hear that it still had that name. Sharing meals with her in this Pug's Parlour were the butler, the valet, the lady's maid and the cook. Albert had his meals with the servants in the servants' hall – he wasn't allowed in with the hierarchy.

They made a great fuss of him, as they always did when there was a strange man in the house, and one unconnected with domestic work. In spite of being without me for three days, or perhaps because of it, I think Albert enjoyed his stay below stairs.

He got a £2 tip, too, from the lady of the house for being 'such a good and careful packer', so when he came back we were able to have an evening out on some of it. Albert wanted to go to the races and speculate with it. He said he felt lucky – I think those servants had bolstered up his ego. I think too he thought he was really somebody, not the same old Albert who worked for a furniture remover's. I promptly vetoed that. Anyone can see by how prosperous the bookies look that the punters seldom make money. Besides, he might have got bitten by the gambling bug, and as the idea of having a casino in Brighton was being talked about at that time, he might have been tempted to go there. It was going to be at the Metropole, and I couldn't see Albert getting in there. Nevertheless, I was a great believer in nipping in the bud any ideas that my husband got above and beyond the call of duty!

Mind you, it took a long time before the casino came to anything. Like too many of the bright ideas that the Councillors of Brighton and Hove think up. Fortunately, many of them never do materialize, such as the one they had in 1952. They wanted to remove the Clock Tower that's in the middle of Queen's Road. One councillor called it an 'architectural monstrosity'. A lot of old things are architectural monstrosities – so are a lot of old people, but they've got their place, so leave them alone. Anyway, many residents, me included, were enraged at this idea of moving our clock and we made our feelings felt. We knew the real reason was to make it easier for the motorist – and why should everything that's old and traditional have to be destroyed because of motorists? Anyway, it's still stuck there in the middle of the road today, I'm glad to say.

It's always been a source of mirth to me to read about some of the grandiose schemes that get debated at council meetings. About the same time, again, one Hove councillor came up with the idea that Hove should become a Paris-by-the-Sea! To start with, the pubs shut at half past ten in the winter, or eleven o'clock in the summer; there's no night-life of any kind and no transport after about eleven at night. A large percentage of the residents are of retiring age and, though some of them might qualify as models for a *Portrait of an Absinthe Drinker*, like in that picture by Toulouse-Lautrec, their fashions could never be described as other than dowdy. (They did once try having a dress show on the lawns on the promenade, but the howling wind turned it into an underwear display!)

Brighton council, too, got caught up with the idea, and thought about making part of the beach a *plage* – whatever that may mean – 'thus giving Brighton', as they said, 'a gay, Continental air'! *Plage* or no *plage*, the only air you'd get on Brighton front is a gay fish and chips one. And what about our famous Brighton pebbles? Speaking as a resident, one of our favourite sights is to watch the holiday-makers in their bikinis tripping gracefully along the concrete from their beach huts on to the shore and, as their feet hit the pebbles, to see them turn into contorting marionettes. And as for basking comfortably on a mound of stones, which they try to do, can you imagine people doing that in their own back gardens? Anyway, I think it's a mistake to try to emulate Continental countries. Even if we did, English people would still want to go abroad for their holidays. And Continental people wouldn't want to come here to discover a pale imitation of their own country, would they?

There used to be a fresh fish market on Brighton front, but

the council did away with that. As they said, who wants their nostrils assailed by the smell of fresh food today? Nobody. It would be all wrong. People might even find they want to eat fresh food, and that would never do. Get it out of sight. Don't let people see where their fish fingers come from.

There again, still on this Continental lark, we're not people that live in the Continental image. You can't say we're happy, carefree and uninhibited at any rate. For those of us above middle age, it's only when we go abroad that we accept sex and nudity as a natural state of affairs.

I remember on our only trip abroad, the first night Albert and I sat outside a café until three o'clock in the morning drinking something that they called beer – ice-cold the drink was, and so were we. And yet we thought we were really whooping it up. When we got back home we talked about it as if we'd indulged in some form of loose living.

Mind you, this colourful Continental image is a load of cobblers. When we were in Paris, everyone was dressed in grey or black, looking like miniature de Gaulles, dropping their *nons* all over the place and talking about *le bombe* as if it had fallen on them. The newspaper sellers, who in England add a bit of brightness and colour to the scene, went around calling out '*Le Monde*' as if it had just come to an end. Talk about Gay Paree and the Entente Cordiale!

But back to the job in hand – charring. When Mr Hardmore died I'd reached a sort of impasse. I knew that I'd have difficulty replacing him. In any case, Albert wasn't exactly dead keen that I should work for another man, so I got a job with a Mr and Mrs Cohen, who lived in a big block of flats. Fortunately, I was warned about her because the morning I started there I went up in the lift with another char who worked in a different flat. 'Hello, ducks,' she said, 'you're a stranger – never seen you here before.' I said, 'No, I'm just starting.' 'Who're you working for?' 'Mrs Cohen.' Then she groaned, 'Oh Gawd, you'll never stick her for long – every char in this building has worked for her. She's a tartar!'

She was. She was an impossible person to work for. She couldn't help it, she had a fetish about cleanliness. All orthodox Jews are particular – you have to use different tea cloths for drying different kinds of utensils and do a variety of things in certain ways. But she had a fetish for *cleaning*: every single month the whole kitchen had to be washed – the walls and the ceiling. All the china had to be washed. I even had to wash the boot brushes once a week. So after I'd been there a few weeks, Mother had to break her leg again.

All the time I was working for Mrs Cohen I was scanning the newspapers for another job – preferably outside house-work, because after my experience with her I really felt I needed a change from it. Then I happened to see an advertise-ment asking for part-time interviewers for a social survey. I knew it would only be a temporary job. It was to find out what people did with their spare time.

Now here was a conscience teaser. There I had been all my life going on about nosy parkers prying into other people's lives, invading their privacy, and now I found myself tempted to become one of them myself. And I gave way to the temp-tation. It's the old story – it's easy enough to criticize other people, but when faced with a similar circumstance yourself, you do exactly as they did. It's been on my conscience a bit since, because these social surveys take me back to when I was young, and the upper class used to come round and tell the poor how to live on thirty shillings a week, when it's only the people who have to live on thirty shillings a week that know how to do it.

I went for an interview and got offered the job, and I accepted. What really made me take it was that I thought it'd be a step up in the social scale. If people asked what I did I could say I was a researcher; it sounded good to me – better than saying I was a char, anyway. And I found when I was talking to people that I brought the conversation round to what I was doing and I made it sound ever so important. I suppose I'm just a snob at heart. Mind you, I didn't try it on my family. I know what I'd have got from them! Another reason I took it was that I'd have to do a lot of talking and I like talking.

There were half a dozen of us to do the town. Before we started we had about an hour's briefing on how to ask the questions. For instance, if we were calling on working-class people, we were told to be hail-fellow-well-met; if it was a semi-detached area, we were to adopt a kind of nice way of speaking, you see – not subservient, but *nice*; and if we visited anyone higher in the social scale, we were to adopt a kind of 'Well, I know you're doing me a great big favour, but this is my living and I really do need someone to help me do it' manner. I'm sure it was the right way to do it, but I had my own ideas and I wanted to try them out first. I was allotted a working-class district in the beginning. I knocked on my first door and when it was opened, said, 'I wonder if I could interest you ...' I never got any further – the woman promptly said, 'Not today, thank you,' and shut the door.

The next one I tried, I started, 'A social survey is being done in this neighbourhood ...' Well, from the expression that came over her face, you'd have thought I'd spat in her eye. 'Alf!' she bawled out, 'there's a bloody council snooper down here!' Then she said to me, 'I suppose what you want to know is what we earn, how we earn it, what we spend it on and everything else that's none of your business.' I murmured something about 'leisure', then Alf shouted, 'What's the bitch on about?' 'She wants to know what you do in your spare time!' So he bellowed back, 'Tell her what you always tell me – I'm a layabout, I do bugger-all and she can bugger off!' I did. And speedily. I've never been out of a porch so quick in my life. Social researcher, I thought to myself – give me the refined life of a char!

The trouble was that I'd started in a council-house district and there's so many things that you're not allowed to do in a council house. Like knocking nails into the walls, keeping pets or taking in lodgers. And in those days, at any rate, people whose family income fell below a certain level were rent-subsidized so they didn't like people coming round and asking questions, and who's to blame them?

Fortunately for me, they weren't all like my first two. Anyway, I changed my initial approach and eventually I was amazed at what people did tell me. Facts that you'd have thought they would have been diffident about confiding to a stranger. Some of them couldn't seem to stop once they got going. They poured out details of their life, and their relatives', friends' and neighbours' lives, in a never-ending stream. In fact, I wasn't considered a good interviewer because I was supposed to do four interviews a session, but I could only get in two; I just couldn't seem to get away.

Widows, I found, were the greatest talkers – not working-class widows because most of them go out to work anyway; the higher-class kind, the sort I used to go out charring for. I suppose they were bored and lonely, very seldom met anyone who wanted them to talk about themselves. All right, they might go out to bridge parties or clubs, but when you're mixing with people they don't want a conversation taken up entirely by what *you* want to say. But I *did*, so it was a wonderful opportunity for them to get it off their chests.

Some people, of course, were just natural talkers, like Mrs Brown. She was a working-class woman and she wasn't bored or lonely. But she welcomed me into her kitchen and poured me out a cup of tea from a huge enamel pot. This tea pot was kept constantly on the stove, and replenished with extra spoonfuls all day long. It tasted like no tea that I've ever had before or since. I shuddered to think what the lining of my stomach was going to be like after swallowing the stuff. I remarked on it to her, 'Do you drink it as strong as this all the time?' She said, 'Yes. Grandad likes it that way.' Grandad was sitting by the fire – he looked about ninety. Well, I thought, he seems to have survived it, so perhaps it won't kill me, and I took another sip. He was smoking one of those old clay pipes, looking reasonably well and still finding life enjoyable. It was obvious from the way Mrs Brown spoke that she, her husband and family, thought the world of Grandad, and I remember thinking how pleasant it was to see somebody really enjoying having an old person with them. I must say, to me he was a rather unlovely sight. He had one large, decayed, blackened tooth sticking right out of the front of his mouth, a bald head, and leathery, grubby skin. But he was a jovial soul and obviously still very much a part of the family.

It appeared his hobby was sending off for the free samples that were advertised in the papers. So I gave him some coupons I had with me for samples of soap and shampoo. Not, as I've said, that he looked as though he washed much. As for the shampoo, it would be no use for his bald head, as I remarked to him. 'I haven't lost *all* my hair everywhere, you know!' he said, and he started wheezing and chuckling. I did a bit of a giggle, but I thought it best not to pursue the subject.

It was difficult interviewing Mrs Brown because she would keep up a constant stream of information about her family. She got out the family album, and I had to sit on the sofa and look through it with her. All of a sudden up pipes Grandad. 'Maudie,' he said, 'tell her about our Ada.' It appeared that 'our Ada' was Mrs Brown's eldest daughter who was now married and living in Canada. During the war a lot of Canadians were stationed in Brighton. Our Ada had got in the family way with a Canadian soldier, who'd gone overseas almost before she knew of her condition.

She tried everything that we knew in those days to get rid of it; mustard baths, quinine, gin, and the old penny-royal pills, but none of them shifted it. According to Mrs Brown, our Ada had got very depressed because she didn't know if she'd see her soldier again. Anyway, Grandad had a very bright idea.

It must have been round about November 5th, Firework Night. Our Ada went to the outside loo. Grandad was waiting for this opportunity. He lit a couple of fireworks – jumping jacks, they were – and slung them under the door. Well, when they went off Ada took fright, jumped up off the seat up in the air, and the shock brought her on. At first she was absolutely livid with rage about it, but, as Grandad said, two tenpenny fireworks were cheaper than a £50 abortion!

Apparently her Canadian soldier was a bit of a rarity – he did come back from France and eventually married our Ada. And he really did live on a ranch, too, but unfortunately for our Ada, he didn't own it, he only worked on it. And by now she was fed up with the wide-open spaces where men are men. According to the letters that she wrote home, she was dying to get back there, but there wasn't the money. Mrs Brown reckoned that if ever our Ada did return to Brighton she'd never go back to Canada.

Just as I was trying finally to say good-bye for the umpteenth time to Mrs Brown and Grandad, Mr Brown came in for his dinner. So Mrs Brown said to him, 'This lady wants to know what you do in your spare time.' 'Oh,' he said, 'just step upstairs and I'll show you.' Well, I'd only just shaken hands with him. I said, 'Do you mind. My husband keeps me busy enough – I'm not putting in overtime!' But it turned out that there was a spare room upstairs that he used for carpentry – making coffee tables and stools and things like that. Was my face red! Grandad went into fits of laughter, of course. I thought he was going to die of apoplexy.

Anyway, we all parted with great friendliness, and Grandad invited me to kiss him good-bye, but in view of his black tooth, his old clay pipe and his grubby appearance, I couldn't face it. I thought Mr Brown might have made the offer after his earlier remark, but he didn't.

What astonished me in this working-class area was the contrast inside of houses that looked the same outside. Some were delightful places, spick and span like little palaces, while others were pig-sties both in appearance and smell. When I found myself in one of the latter kind, I wouldn't sit down, I pretended I was in a hurry and rattled off the questions as quickly as I could. I was doing this one afternoon with an unsavoury little man who'd told me when he answered the door that his wife was busy upstairs. I was about half-way through when a voice shouted down – I suppose it was his wife's – 'Hey, Willie, d'you want a bit of "bod" before I put my corsets on?' I couldn't believe my ears. I didn't know what to do. Then he shouted back, 'Hang on, Eth, I shan't be a minute'; he turned to me and said, 'What's the next question?' as though Eth's remark was the most natural thing in the world. How I got through the rest of the interview I don't know. I'm not easily shaken – but really!

The following week I was given a better-class district. Once again I had difficulty in finding the right initial approach, and quite a lot refused to let me in. But where they were agreeable, the atmosphere was very different from that of the previous week. We'd sit in the lounge drinking tea from dainty cups and munching those thin lunch biscuits, or – though only in one case – we drank sherry, as the house owner said she felt more sociable with drink. I had a hilarious morning there because we did the bottle in and by then it was impossible to know who was interviewing who!

I was finding by now that although it was a well-paid job, you earned your money doing it. At one house the door was opened by Mrs Broom, a woman of about forty. At first she hesitated before she asked me in, and it was very hard getting any sort of information out of her, but when she got going there poured forth more malice and venom than I'd have believed a human being to contain. First she started on the neighbours, who she described as a collection of prigs, prostitutes and parasites. 'There's a house up this road,' she said, 'where the milkman stays over half an hour. What's he doing all that time – milking the old cow?'

Then she went on, 'How can the women in this street afford to dress the way they do on their husbands' wages? I'll tell you what they do,' she said, 'they make it from other men on the sly. And what's more, their husbands encourage them to do it. Husbands are beasts. All men are beasts.' Then she went on to tell me she'd been married twice; that her second husband had left her six months ago; that she was in a highly nervous condition and was having psychiatric treatment. 'But,' she said, 'the doctor's a man and therefore a beast and is in league against me!' What could I do with anyone like that? I'm not unsympathetic. I know that mental illness is a very real and harrowing complaint, but I certainly wished myself anywhere but in that house.

Yet short of being blatantly rude, I had to stay and listen to her. I had to hear why her first marriage had failed – it hadn't been her fault, of course. She was pure and a virgin when she married and she knew nothing about 'all that', so the honeymoon was a revolting experience, ruined by 'all that', and since then she'd never been able to do with 'all that'.

Apparently, after ten years of misery, Cecil, her husband, let her divorce him. Well, you'd have thought after her experience she'd have said Good-bye to All That, but no, she got married again. I murmured my astonishment. 'Ah,' she said, 'but Alan, my second husband, he seemed different, not a ravenous beast like Cecil!' Unfortunately, Alan, according to

Mrs Broom, had sexual desires of a nature she couldn't bring herself to speak about. She put her marriage failures down to the fact that she wasn't good in bed.

I do get a bit tired of hearing about who is and who is not good in bed. When I was young, any working-class husband would have been highly suspicious of a wife who was immediately 'good in bed' – he would have wondered where she acquired her techniques.

But it's always the woman's fault if that side of marriage is a failure. It's never the man's. Men have got far more chance to get experience, nobody blames a man if he's sampled it far and wide. When I was in the marriage market, anyone who got a man who had sampled it far and wide and managed to marry him was considered to have made a good catch. She'd got him to the altar when nobody else could.

I think that Mrs Broom's troubles could partly have been solved if she'd drunk a bit. She took pains to tell me she was a teetotaller. Drinking does loosen your inhibitions – well, I've found it does. It makes you feel in love with all the world and as you can't make love with all the world, you settle for the partner you've got.

As I've said, being a researcher was a job with its hazards. At another house where I called the door was opened by a man, and when I asked to see his wife he said she wasn't in. Now, we'd been warned about this. We were told if there was only a man in the house, not to go in. But this one said his wife had gone to the corner shop, she'd be back in a minute and he knew that she'd be pleased to take part in a social survey. I could see he had a wife, because the house showed every sign of a woman being around.

I'd been there about twenty minutes and his wife hadn't shown up. The man was a sort of short, fat, rather pathetic-looking creature, with pendulous cheeks that moved up and down, wobbling like a jelly every time he spoke, and as he was a compulsive talker I became hypnotized by them. He offered me a drink, which I refused because I found the fumes that came from him were intoxicating enough. I settled for a cup of tea.

While we were drinking this he swallowed a couple of pills.

Well, I thought, he's probably got a headache or it's some sort of prescription, but with a meaningful look he said that they were 'potency pills'. I was immediately on my guard. Then he went on to say that he'd seen them advertised in a magazine and that they were very good. I knew the ones he meant though I'd never answered the ad, but I'd thought about it. They had them in three strengths, and they were for women whose husbands weren't much good in bed. You see, now I've caught the phrase! It was suggested that the wives put them in their husbands' beverage last thing at night. They wouldn't know you had because the pills were tasteless. I could never understand why there were three strengths. I suppose the strongest were the most expensive. You bought them, dropped them into your husband's drink, waited a moment and then you both galloped upstairs like mad. It used to make me laugh to think of this treble strength! What sort of husband needed treble strength?

I wasn't laughing now, though – I was thinking fast. He didn't get aggressive, just maudlin. That must have been the drink. He got up from his chair and sat down on the sofa next to me and sighed. I didn't like to show distaste, I didn't want to hurt his feelings, but when he started off saying, 'I think a man is as old as he feels,' I said to myself, Here, wait for it, gal, you've heard that gambit before! It was when I took up old-time dancing before I was married. I used to go regularly, and often got ancient men – or what seemed to me then ancient men – as partners.

I remember one who'd got such a corporation that he kept me rolling off my feet on it while I danced with him! He bought me a drink in the interval, and then during the next dance he said, 'Do you think I'm too old to dance?' Well, naturally, with my aversion to hurting anyone's feelings – well, he'd spent a shilling on a port for me and I was looking for another, so I said, 'Oh no, not too old for old-time dancing, anyway.' 'Ah,' he said, trotting out this same gambit, 'a man is as old as he feels,' and his hands began to do just that over me. I quickly abandoned him, I can assure you. I didn't mind dancing on a corporation for a port or two, but I didn't want the storm afterwards.

So when this chap came out with the same remark, and was edging nearer and nearer to me on the sofa, I thought it behoved me to use some strategy. So I said to him, 'You know, you're lucky to have such good health. The reason why I'm doing this work is because mine is so poor. I've got constantly to be out in the fresh air.' 'Oh,' he said, 'have you? Why, what's the matter with you?' I said sadly, 'The doctors don't seem to know. They've given me all sorts of tests, but they don't *think* it's contagious ...' The speed with which he removed himself from the sofa in other circumstances would have been unflattering. And when, after another few minutes, I said, 'Well, it doesn't look as if your wife is coming back, does it? I think I'll make a call elsewhere,' he made no effort whatsoever to detain me.

The job finished after three weeks, that was the extent of it, and I wasn't sorry. It had been a bit of a strain getting the right sort of information. Mind you, I salved my conscience by thinking, All right, I may have invaded their privacy, but some of them tried to invade mine! I also found that quite a lot of people positively welcomed my inquiries into how they lived. Some of them were even sorry that there weren't more questions to answer. I can only put it down to the fact that their lives were so empty and pointless that even to answer my queries made them feel real people again. It made them feel important to think that anyone was interested enough to want to know something of their lives. One middle-aged and quite well-to-do widow assured me that she always filled in every form sent to her by the council or the government, 'because,' she said, 'for a brief while it gives me the feeling that I'm alive and my existence is noted somewhere. Otherwise every day is so much like another that I could be in a dream and not in a real world at all.'

To my amazement, when the survey was over I was asked if I would join full-time and do them in other towns. It must have been that although I didn't do as many interviews as some of the others did, because I talked too much and listened too long to other people, I got masses of information and information that they needed. But of course I couldn't go to another town. The beauty of the job to me had been that it was part-time, in my home town, well paid and, above all, a complete change.

I never did discover what this social survey was in aid of. And when I was able to think about it in retrospect, I wondered – do people tell complete strangers the truth, or do they project a sort of image of what they'd like to be, not what they really are? An image of how they'd like the world to see them, and maybe how they'd like to see the world?

I went back to charring with the feeling that I'd seen a slice of life, made two or three permanent friends, and also I got a jolly good job through it. At one place where I called they'd got a 'daily' who was having to leave because her husband's firm had moved him to another town, and she informed me, with tears in her eyes, that her employers were the most wonderful people to work for, and that she was heartbroken to be leaving them. I accepted what she said with some reservations, especially as, over the cup of tea I had with her, she'd told me she'd been to the local cinema and the film had made her weep buckets; anyone that can weep buckets over a film could weep at anything! Still, I took the job.

9

ABOUT this time I had a visit from my old friend Vi, the Mrs Davis who I had been friends with when I went down to Hove after Albert's call-up. She'd gone back to Stepney, where her husband, Alf, was a docker, after the war. I look back on that Sunday afternoon, when Vi, Alf and their two youngest children called on me with terrible guilt feelings, because I greeted them with such dismay. The reason was that by now two of my sons were at grammar school and the other at university, and I felt there was a great gulf between them and Vi's children. Then again, I was trying to copy the way my sons spoke – I don't mean in my accent, I've never been able to alter that, but in the content of what I said. I was no longer as bawdy or down-to-earth as Vi was, not outwardly, anyway.

Vi, of course, was still the same, only more so. She'd had a sort of refresher course in bawdiness by going back to Stepney. So, for the first half-hour of their visit things were very hard going.

It's no good trying to cover it up, I was a snob. I didn't like it, but I couldn't help it. I made them welcome, with tea and everything, but there wasn't that sort of outgoing friendliness that there'd been when Vi and I first met. Albert wasn't there, fortunately, he was upstairs having his usual Sunday afternoon snooze, otherwise I think it would have been even worse.

Anyway, there were no flies on Vi, she wasn't just all beer and b's, because when she saw a photo of my eldest son in his university gown, she said, 'Oh my, we have come up in the world, haven't we?' Then she went on with a sniff, 'My kids never made the grade, but it wasn't because they're stupid, they were deprived!' It's one of the regular clichés now, isn't it, to enable people to accept failure or misfortune? Nothing today is ever called by its right name. When I went to school, the idle or stupid children were called lazy nitwits; now they're 'culturally deprived'. Similarly, there are no poor or shiftless families, they're underprivileged or deprived. It *sounds* better, it makes the government and the do-gooders feel that they've achieved something if they call them by a different name. Unlike the rose, if you call shiftless and poor people 'underprivileged', it gives them a lift-up in the social scale. It's better to be underprivileged than to be poor, just as it's better to be a refuse collector than a dustman, or a rodent operator than a rat-catcher. To my way of thinking, it's better still to have the money and the position.

It turned out that Vi and Alf were down to see what the work situation was like for Alf in Brighton and Hove. My heart sank lower and lower at the prospect of them being down permanently. I had visions of them as neighbours again. I was able to tell them – and it was true – that there was a lot of unemployment in the town, particularly out of season, and I said to Alf, 'Why do you want to leave the docks anyway?' Vi never gave him time to answer – Vi never did give him time to answer – she said, 'He desn't want to leave but he's just had an operation on his prostate and the doctor says he's not to do any heavy work.'

Poor old Alf – he had to sit there and listen to all the details of his operation, how it had affected his sexual performance, and how frustrated Vi got, and she ended by saying, 'He doesn't seem to care for it any more.' Oh dear! I could feel myself coming out in hot flushes. Not that Alf minded. He just sat there as though it was a normal thing to talk about. It may have been that because his organ, as Vi called it, couldn't work, he liked to think it served some purpose, even if only as a conversation piece!

Another reason that Vi wanted to come down was that they'd moved from their old house in Stepney to a flat in one of the council blocks, and Vi didn't like it at all. She missed having neighbours and talking over the garden wall with them. 'It's not the same in a block,' she said. 'It's nothing but swarms of kids on the landings and in the lift. It's like a bloody circus!'

Although I didn't enjoy Vi's visit, it did me a good turn, because I was able to get rid of a monstrosity of a hall-stand that we had in our passage. I'd acquired this object at an auction sale. I'd gone there just for fun – I didn't expect to make a bid. It was the first I'd ever been to. I went because friends were always telling me what marvellous bargains they'd picked up. 'Wait till the end,' they said, 'let the dealers have what they want, and you can often buy a gem.' The things they showed me seemed all right, so I thought I'd go along just to see what the form was the first time. Then this enormous hall-stand appeared, with two drawers, a large mirror, a place for umbrellas and antlers for hanging hats and coats on. It looked as though a herd of deer were sticking their necks through it. Talk about Stag at Bay! I reckon the Stag's entire harem had been decapitated and fitted on this hall stand.

The auctioneer said, 'How much am I bid for this fine old piece?' and he was greeted with hearty laughter all round. Somebody said, 'Five bob'. And all of a sudden there was a voice saying, 'Ten shillings!' and it was mine. Well, nobody raised the bid, and there was I, the owner of this object, originally designed for some baronial hall. I was horrified. I knew what Albert would say, he'd say I'd absolutely gone round the bend – and he did. Incidentally, I had to give a man another five bob to get the thing home. And when he got it into our passage there was just room to squeeze by – you had to duck your head under the antlers otherwise they would have gouged your eyes out. Talk about the horns of a dilemma!

Albert sawed off some of the antlers eventually, but even so it was a snare and a delusion. That was the first and only time I ever went to an auction sale!

Vi had always coveted this monstrosity, and I'd offered to give it to her, but she'd only ever had a passage like mine. Now, in these new flats, she had a hall, so not only did she give me ten bob for it, she even paid to have it transported up to London. I was highly delighted.

Then the conversation got round to my work and Vi said, 'Are you still going out charring?' I told her I was and also described the social survey I'd been doing. She said, 'You want to do one of those in Stepney. Let me know if you do and I'll give you some addresses!'

I heaved a sigh of relief when Vi, Alf and the children went, though I was left with terrible feelings of remorse at having discovered that I was as much of a snob as many of the people I had despised for being one. I sometimes think it's the faults in yourself that you most dislike in other people.

This couple that I was working for, Mr and Mrs Grant, believed in spiritualism, and once a week they went to a séance. It was as a result that I got an extra afternoon's work as well as a glimpse of the occult world.

These spiritualist meetings were run by a Mrs Cotter, who called herself Madame Tara. She needed someone to prepare and serve tea after the séance, so I went along. She paid me ten shillings a time, and as I wasn't there very long and shared in the séance and wasn't treated as a servant, this was good enough for me. And I liked her. She was a large, bosomy lady. When she went out she wore a flowing black cloak caught up in front by a brooch in the shape of a yellow spider, and this with her pillarbox-red lips and two hectic spots of rouge on her cheeks made her conspicuous even in a town like Hove, where oddity is the rule rather than the exception.

Though, as I say, she looked odd, she wasn't grotesque, but more imposing and sort of deep, as though there was a lot to her – I mean apart from her build.

She was extravagant and expansive in her speech, too. 'Oh Mrs Powell, I've lived life to the full. I've dwelt on Parnassus and plumbed the Stygian waters of human iniquity,' she said to me shortly after I began working there. Exactly what she meant by that, or whether there was any truth in it, I never found out. She only had one strange disability: she was always burping. Her conversations were punctuated with Pardon Me's.

I must say her surroundings, apart from the exotic atmosphere of the room where the séances took place, gave no indication of a life in any way out of the ordinary. The séance room smacked of the East, with its tapestries and drapes. There were photographs of a motley collection of people whom Madame Tara described as 'grateful friends', and there were silver mementoes of varying kinds inscribed to 'Dear Leonie', which I presumed was her Christian name; on one silver salver was just written 'To one who has heard' – very cryptic!

The photos of her husband, who had 'passed over', were confined to the other rooms in the house. I could see the reason for this, because he had what I thought was a wall-eye, but which Madame Tara told me later was in fact a glass eye. In one photo his real eye looked straight ahead while the glass one, like the eye of a stuffed bird, followed me round the room. So if I was ever tempted to remove a cigarette from one of the boxes, I always felt that that eye was on me and I'd take my hand away. This was probably as well because my instinct told me that Madame Tara counted the cigarettes every morning!

Her husband had died when he was comparatively young, about fifty. Apparently he drank and was what she called accident prone; he'd lost his left arm when he was a young man, then later his right leg had to be amputated below the knee, his eye had gone in a pub brawl, and two fingers of his right hand had been sliced off in some machine. After she'd told me this I felt like saying, 'It's as well he went when he did – if he'd lived much longer there'd have been precious little left to bury!'

There was a young French au pair girl, Denise, who used to help me with the teas. A very pretty girl, she was over here to learn the language because her father kept a hotel in France and she was going to work for him, so she talked to me as much as possible to help her with her English. When I told Albert this, he said she must have been out of her mind. Even Albert can show a nasty streak from time to time.

In my conversations with her, I asked this Denise if she'd got a boy-friend in France. She fairly bubbled over at this and showed me several photos of him. Then I asked about his work. 'Oh,' she said, ' 'e ees – 'ow you call 'im? – an erection engineer.' I know I must have a peculiar mind, but I couldn't help thinking as I looked at her pretty face that he'd have little difficulty engineering one of those with Denise around.

I was never able to discover whether Madame Tara took money for these spiritual get-togethers or not. I imagine she must have, because although the believers spent the afternoon hovering in those ethereal regions, it didn't seem to affect their appetites once they came back to earth – they drank tea and devoured sandwiches and cakes as though they'd been on a ten-mile hike!

Madame Tara, although she wasn't a medium, seemed to have some kind of extra-sensory power. I remember once when I was putting the chairs into the séance room, which, incidentally, was the only work I was allowed to do in there, she turned to me and said, 'Yes, Mrs Powell, I'm sure you'll be able to get away from here in time to go and see your mother' – which was just what I had been wondering at that moment, and I hadn't ever mentioned my mother to her. Another time, it was during the tea-drinking after the séance, she used the ouija board – it's a sort of thing that writes under its own steam, or some sort of occult steam, and the pencil wrote a message from a member of the circle who was in America to say that she would be with them next week, and this was a month earlier than she'd expected to return. And she was.

I'd always imagined that mediums were sort of ascetic, out-of-this-world people, but *our* medium was very much of it: a plump, ordinary-looking middle-aged woman. But, as Madame Tara explained to me, the medium didn't do things through her own personality, it was her alter ego, or contact, that took over.

Our medium's contact was a *hadji*. This *hadji* had died immediately after making a pilgrimage to Mecca. Since he'd had no time to commit any sins after the pilgrimage, he was in a state of beatitude, which enabled him to get through easily, as no earthly materialism intervened between him and the medium. This sounded impressive whether it meant anything or not.

At the first séance I attended there were about twelve of us present. The room was in darkness except for a dim electric light high on the wall which flickered in a very mysterious manner. We all had to hold hands. I'd got Denise on one side of me and a rather elderly man on the other. Suddenly, the medium went rigid, and called out, 'Where are you, Abdul? Come in, Abdul. Are you there, Abdul?' I was thrilled at first, but after she'd said this about half a dozen times I got a bit fed up, and I whispered to Denise, 'I expect he's in Mecca sitting this dance out!' Fortunately, Denise didn't understand a word I said, otherwise we'd both of us have started giggling and I giggle loudly.

Soon after this, though, Abdul did come in, and quite a different voice came out of the medium. It was like an old man's voice, and her fingers began to shine. All right, I realised afterwards that it could have been luminous paint on the tips of her fingers, but I was impressed at the time. The medium, speaking in this *hadji*'s voice, said, 'There's a man here and his name begins with a C and he wants to remind one of us—' She stopped for a bit, and then, 'Her name begins with—' there was a lot of mumbling and then loud and clear – 'her name begins with R. C wants to ask R if she remembers the little Swiss valley where, together, they ate the cream cakes.' I found this a bit of an anti-climax after the big consti-pated build-up, but there was a shout from one of the circle – her name was Rose – 'Oh,' she said, 'it's my husband Cyril

111

trying to reach me! Yes, yes! Tell him I remember the place very well!'

Everyone got very excited at this. It was all fine and dandy, but they all knew, including the medium, that Rose and her dear departed had gone to Switzerland every year for their holiday, and it was old history that Rose always made a bee-line for the cream cakes at tea-time! So the medium knew that she was on to something for nothing, didn't she, when she came out with this one?

The only other member of the circle that got a message that day was a woman whose recently dead great-aunt wanted to give her instructions about some money she'd left her. It just showed, didn't it, that it doesn't pay to be rich – you go on worrying about money even after you're dead. In any case, this great-aunt had lived in Worthing, which is ten miles from Brighton, and was buried there. It was a pity she couldn't have got in spiritual touch with her grand-niece from there, instead of going all the way to Abdul and back. I suppose it was an early form of these satellite messages.

At my next – and last – séance there were about sixteen of us, tightly packed round the table. No sooner had the lights gone out when the table gave a terrific lurch. Great excitement reigned until it was discovered that it was only the dyspeptic, fifteen-stone Madame Tara giving one of her earth-shaking belches! Soon after this the medium went into what seemed to me more a state of catalepsy than a trance – she went rigid, then rolled about moaning, and actually foamed at the mouth, though I've since heard that foaming can be induced with the aid of a special tablet. The medium pops it in her mouth before you go in, then she foams. Next there was all this calling again for Abdul, and Abdul seemed to be a long way away.

Eventually he came through, with an incoherent message from somebody who had apparently been transported on a convict ship to Australia. He was now in Purgatory and wanted a relative who was in our circle to pray for him, but as no one there wanted to acknowledge such a low-class relation, Abdul was told to leave him in Purgatory.

Then, after great travail from the medium, there came through a message for one Dora. Abdul's voice said, 'This is for Dora – remember the 14th.' There was a silence, then it repeated, 'Remember the 14th.' Suddenly there was a hair-raising scream and a thud as one of the circle fell forward on the table in a faint.

Everyone rushed to put the lights on, and we found it was a new member, a young woman of about twenty-five. When she'd recovered, she told us that she'd just moved down from the Midlands, that she was to have been married the year before on April 14th, but two days before the wedding her fiancé was killed in a car accident. She went on to say that the reason she'd moved to Brighton was to get away from every-thing that reminded her of the tragedy.

I must say I was duly impressed by this, and yet later I thought, Why had she come to a séance unless she was hoping to get in touch with the dead, and who was she likely to want to hear from except her fiancé?

Of course, Madame Tara was overjoyed at the success of this séance. 'Ah,' she said, 'God moves in a mysterious way.' To my mind he mostly moves in a highly improbable way!

That was the last séance that I was allowed to attend. Mad-ame Tara said that the medium could sense that I was hostile and thus prevented the contact from getting through. She wasn't annoyed or anything; she went on to say that my 'aura' radiated disbelief in Abdul and he couldn't get past me. Well, I could see how terrible it was that this poor *hadji*, after hav-ing travelled all the way from Mecca, found his way blocked by little me. Mind you, I don't think I'm psychic in any way at all. I remember in one of the houses I was working in in service, the servants spread it around that the drawing-room was haunted by the ghost of a young sweep who'd got himself suffocated up the chimney there – the Charles Kingsley's *Water Babies* lark. I was dared to go down there at night with a candle and wait around in case if I could see it. I went, but never felt a breath of a ghost, nor was I afraid. It's not that I'm brave, it's just that I find there are enough mortal things to be frightened of for me to worry about the immortal.

Although I wasn't allowed to attend these séances, I went on making tea for them, and about four weeks after the Dora episode the medium failed to arrive for the séance. Madame

Tara had tried to contact her but she'd not been able to. The following week my employers told me that, for the time being, the circle had stopped meeting. They didn't want to talk about it, but I kept on at them. Eventually it came out that this medium had been extorting money from one of the members, a widow. She'd got away with most of her money, and her family were taking proceedings against her.

Well, of course, I could see that it was easy for a clever and unscrupulous medium to prey on a person with a credulous nature by giving them 'messages' from someone that they'd loved, telling them what to do with their money, then pocketing the lot themselves.

It all seems so absurd, doesn't it, that anyone could be taken in by this kind of thing? I'd thought so myself before I'd attended these meetings, but it comes down to the fact that people will believe what they want to believe. Even after this eye-opener, the people I was doing 'daily' work for and who'd introduced me to Madame Tara, still continued with spiritualism. They say love is blind. Maybe it is, but it's much more rewarding than some of the other things that seem to affect people's eyesight.

10

ALTHOUGH I was still pursuing culture, I found that going out to work and trying to run my own home at the same time, with no mechanical aids like washing machines or vacuum cleaners, was a real hindrance in acquiring an intellectual life. By the time the evening came I was generally so tired that I felt like skipping the classes, though when I got there I very soon livened up – mentally, at any rate.

Despite hearing it quite often on the radio, I'd never been able to enjoy classical music. I felt I must be missing out, so one Sunday I went to a concert at the Dome in Brighton. I knew I hadn't got what people call an ear for music. I've always been tone deaf, but I liked light tunes, such as Strauss and Lehár. I was very Palm Court Orchestra. I thought that listening to this symphony orchestra in the flesh might give me an understanding of the intellectual stuff. I was wrong. I was bored to distraction. I sat through it without understanding or appreciation. As for the singer, she was a soprano. She sang two songs in German, but if they'd been in English it'd have made no difference as far as I was concerned, because I can never make out a word a soprano sings. They warble away on high and nothing but noise gets through to me. I suppose you don't have to worry about the words, it's just the sound of the voice soaring away like a lark – personally I'd sooner listen to a lark any day of the week than a soprano.

And it's not as if they're much to look at. Well, that's not strictly true, there's generally plenty of them. I suppose by the very nature of singing their chests get a lot of exercise, so that as they expand them they get stuck like it – sort of permanently big-chested. This may not matter too much at a concert but it gets ludicrous in opera, especially where they're supposed to be small, appealing and fragile. In plays you sometimes see the hero carrying the heroine in his arms; in opera I can well imagine it being the other way round.

In the interval of this particular concert, the person next to me turned to me and started talking about this singer: what she'd heard her sing before, and where. Then she said, 'Hasn't she got a marellous range? And what attack!' I thought it was supposed to be a concert, not a war. Then she said, 'And her tonal quality – well, there's absolutely no comparison, is there?' Since she didn't tell me who the comparison was with, it was all right, I thought, to agree with her – I wouldn't be letting myself in for anything that way. I suppose it did mean something to her, but I found her like those people who appreciate pictures. They stand back and talk about the perspective, the line, the balance, the harmony, the form – all that sort of malarky, and half the time you can sense they don't know what they're talking about: they've just got these phrases out of a book.

But don't think I'm knocking the real music lovers, it's the phonies I can't stand. I know that there's something lacking in me but I console myself by thinking that no one can fully appreciate the great arts unless they've had some kind of training in their appreciation. I think I can appreciate books, even erudite books like Marcel Proust's *Remembrance of Things Past*. I've read it three times even though it was in twelve volumes. I enjoyed it because not only have I read books all my life but I've been taught how to read them. I go round art galleries, and I know what I like, but what I like may not necessarily mean that it's a work of art.

I think art appreciation has to be taught too. I don't subscribe to the philosophy of people who say, '*I* know what *I* like and I don't like *that*, therefore it's rubbish.' I can really enjoy good food and I think part of the reason is that I know the ingredients that have gone into making the dishes, the methods that have been used and, in particular, the flavour and aptness of the sauces. After listening to the second half of that concert at the Dome, it became obvious that classical music was not for me.

Albert had come to the same conclusion some time before. That was why he wasn't at the concert with me. I'd tried to press him to come but he said there was no point in two people suffering, he was going to settle for a quiet nap at home preserving his strength to console me for an evening mis-spent. Albert says his favourite tune is *Orpheus in the Underground*. That's the way he likes it and that's the way it's going to be.

As I was leaving the concert I was surprised to be spoken to by an elderly lady. 'Are you not Margaret Langley who was my cook when I lived in London?' she said in a loud, authoritative voice. I was furious. Everyone turned and looked at me. It wasn't that I was ashamed of having been a cook, it was the manner in which she spoke, the same way she always had when I'd worked for her, as though I was her slave. And I felt it was intended for all to hear so that they should know that once upon a time she lived in a palace with a retinue of servants. Her manner was *gracious*, as if to say, Look how democratic I'm being, talking to one of my ex-workers. There was nothing riled me more than this segregation of the working class as though we were a kind of entity frozen into a group that never changed no matter what else might. The thing that infuriated me was her very evident surprise at seeing me at a concert of

116

classical music, and then of course, inevitably, she said it: 'I didn't know that you liked music and attended *concerts*.' I half expected her to add 'Cook' in the way she used to.

This did it for me. I drew myself up. 'Madam,' I said (I hadn't called anybody that for years but now I used it derisively), 'when I worked for you you never showed any interest in our likes and dislikes. Your only concern was to get as much work out of us for as little money as possible. And now you mourn for the good old days – but perhaps it was your kind who destroyed them by the way you treated the likes of me. I'm sure you're not a bit interested in me, I'm just a reminder of your past glory. I hope now that I'm an unpleasant reminder!' I then swept off, boiling all the way home, and took it out on Albert because I knew I'd been rude and let myself down. I couldn't help it; I think it did me good to get it off my chest. I'd been putting up with her sort of cant for years, and I'd recently been reminded of it by an article in our local paper.

This was about a council estate where a supermarket was refused a licence to sell alcohol because some do-gooders said that the sort of people who lived there gave beer to their children. What's more they were setting up bars in their kitchens, and getting their babies to sleep by putting gin or brandy in their milk! Of all the unctuous nonsense! I expect the most they had was a couple of bottles of beer in the kitchen cupboard, and the 'bar' was the kitchen table. As for a drop of brandy in the babies' milk, I've seen that done in many places I've worked in. I've been a 'daily' in luxury flats where there were cocktail cabinets full of every drink under the sun – you name it and they had it. Yet because the owners don't live on council estates they can drink themselves under the table and nobody must interfere with them. They can give their children any drink and you mind your own business. What I would have liked to see was some big headlines: *Wealthy estate of ranch-type houses refused drink licence*. I'd even electioneer under a banner like that, and the way I feel about any sort of politics or politicians, that's saying a lot.

I was also particularly sensitive at the time to this kind of thing because the Mrs Rutherford-Smith I'd been working for

117

for some months as a 'daily' was snobbery personified. She didn't know she was – snobs never do – she thought she was being nice, kind and gracious. Her early married name had been just Smith, but when her aunt died leaving her a lot of money on condition that she added the old family name of Rutherford, she did so with alacrity.

I said to her, 'Didn't Mr Smith mind?' 'Oh no,' she said, 'he was a great admirer of my aunt.' That's as may be, he was dead so I couldn't confirm it, but it's my bet it was her money he really admired.

This Mrs R-S said about her aunt that she kept to the old ways of life, common materialism was never allowed to enter it. The aunt lived in a feudal style in her large country house and it was said as though this was some sort of Utopian way of life. I'd read enough history to know what in fact it meant – near slavery.

I could tell from the moment I started working for Mrs R-S that she was constantly aware of the indignity of conversing with a char, yet she had such a strong desire to recall the past that she had to surrender to it. She gave me all the guff about the plight of the landed gentry, the ruinous taxation, the mistake of educating the working class. She spoke of the Welfare State as if it was a Hades of Fire and Brimstone. Everything today was grants, she said, grants for this and grants for that, as though they were passports to purgatory. When I pointed out to her that my sons were being educated on government grants and using them to advantage, she conceded that there might be *some* exceptions. But as she said it I could see that she was only losing face to keep a char.

She was never very explicit about where the Rutherfords had lived or how they had originally made their money, so one day I asked her if it had been as a result of the Industrial Revolution. I stepped right in it there. Their family and financial roots had been in the land. It had been through the Industrial Revolution that they had lost their money. The then-reigning heir, known as Get-Rich-Quick Rutherford, had speculated in mills and factories, with disastrous results. He had no knowledge or understanding of finance and it was he who had ruined the family. As I said to her, 'He couldn't have ruined your aunt, could he?' 'Oh well,' she said, 'she was from another branch of the Rutherfords – they're a very big family.'

Mind you, Mrs Rutherford-Smith disliked the middle class even more than the working class. All right, the working class might have taken these 'grants' and gone on strike, but they didn't ape the manners and behaviour of the aristocracy. According to her, the middle class were 'parvenus and up-starts' who considered themselves rightful heirs to the landed gentry. Although she didn't use the word, I could tell she thought of them as bastards one and all.

Working for her was a bore with her constant saga of the Rutherfords, and me having to watch my p's and q's not to put my foot in it.

Another thing that didn't endear her in my eyes was that she was a dog-lover. She had a Pekinese – Henry. Henry had always been the name for the dog in their family. As soon as one died and they got another, it was called Henry. It re-minded me of that old music hall song beginning 'Every one was an 'Enery' and ending ' 'Enery the Eighth I am'.

I must say that this Henry, in colour, looks and corpulence, was the image of the king who made such a business of matrimony. Not that he was allowed to go in for that sort of thing. There would have been no suitable mates in Brighton for the Rutherford Henry.

Personally, give me cats every time. Cats don't expect a lot of affection – they remain aloof and self-sufficient. If you've got a dog and you go on holiday you have to put it in kennels, and all through the holiday one or other member of the family will say, 'I wonder how Rover' – or Rex or whatever the dog's name is – 'is getting on,' and an air of gloom comes over everybody and feelings of guilt at having abandoned him. With cats you never have this, not, that is, with the ordinary English cat – people tell me that the Burmese or Siamese are different, that they're almost human, a trait which could never endear them to me! The last thing I want is something almost human walking around on four legs!

One thing I hated about Henry was having to mince up chicken for his dinner and then go home and eat shin of beef. Despite all the recipes I'd got on how to make delicious and nourishing meals for about half-a-crown, I still preferred chicken.

Mrs Rutherford-Smith explained to me that Pekinese dogs were highly sensitive as they were descended from the royal dogs of China; that they needed every luxury, the best of food, gentle handling and a consistent heat. I couldn't help wondering, as central heating is a comparatively recent invention, how they'd survived in the olden days!

Contrary to the general opinion that dogs know when a person doesn't like them, this Henry was unaware of my views. He courted my company and would follow me round the flat getting himself tangled in the flex of the vacuum cleaner or chasing round with the hand brush. One of his favourite tricks was to sit on the flex and, when I tugged it towards me, he'd shoot up in the air, turn a somersault and land on his back. At first I thought that he sat on it accidentally, but he did it so often that I'm sure he enjoyed this levitation. I think Henry was sick of the drooling and fondling that he got from Mrs R-S and enjoyed the rough and tumble he had with me.

An idiosyncrasy of Mrs R-S's, though I thought it another indication of her snobbery, was that she had two girls call at the flat to do her hair each week, because she didn't like going to the shop and mixing with the common herd. She hadn't minded going to a hairdresser when there were separate cubicles, but since there were now open-planned rooms where everyone sat around together under the hairdryers she didn't care for it. 'When you've been accustomed to privacy all your life,' she said, 'it's hard to surrender.' So she paid her ransom money to have the hairdressers come to her. Every week she would show me off to these girls. 'Mrs Powell,' she'd call from the bedroom, and in I'd go, 'have you polished the silver?' or 'Will you please lay out the Coalport' – meaning the china dinner service – 'I have guests tonight.' Things she would never ask me ordinarily, and all for the sake of impressing those giggling girls who were messing about with what was left of her hair.

One day when I was hoovering the sitting-room she called me in and said, 'Mrs Powell, I would rather you brushed the Persian rugs with a hand brush; I think I've told you the hoover doesn't do them any good.' I saw the two girls giggling and that did it. I was so fuming with rage, I said, 'The way those two do your hair doesn't do anything for you either – you'd be just as well off bald!' It was a dreadful thing to say, but I was really incensed. With that I walked out of the room.

From the look on Mrs R-S's face I thought I'd had my cards. But such was the state of the domestic market that even a tarnished treasure, as I was now, had a value.

A few days after this episode she said to me, 'Mrs Powell, I have decided to forget what you said to me the other day, but perhaps you would do something for me in return – call me Madam.' Well, I had the greatest difficulty not to laugh. I was reminded not only of that film *Call Me Madam*, but also of an old morality picture that my mother had in her parlour: it showed a poor ragged woman peering through the window of a mansion at a little coffin, and the caption read, 'Dead – and never called me Mother!' My mother had got it from Sunday School years ago, and it had always impressed me as a child, even though I didn't understand what it meant.

Anyway, I was now fed up to the teeth with her, so I said, 'I'm sorry, I've spent many years on domestic staffs and I reckon I've done my share of madaming. My not using the word doesn't mean I have any less respect for you, it's just that it reminds me of a life I was glad to get away from.' 'All right, Mrs Powell,' she said, 'we'll leave it at that, but I'd like to tell you that if I met the Queen I should call her Madam.' What can you say to a woman like that?

Another thing I refused to do was to take Henry out for his lamp-post expeditions. At first she thought I was joking, she couldn't sort of visualize that anyone could deny 'darling Henry' anything. However, when she saw I was adamant, she didn't pursue the matter, so I didn't have to tell her I was employed as a char, not as a dog's lavatory attendant!

On the first Thursday morning of every month, Mrs Rutherford-Smith gave an At Home. Again, she was careful to point out to me that these At Homes bore no resemblance to the At Homes she used to hold, with two parlourmaids dispensing the tea and cakes. I went along to deputize for the two parlourmaids.

Mrs R-S wanted me to dress up in a black frock and fancy apron for these At Homes. In fact she offered to buy them for me. I must say she was a trier. I flatly refused to look like an ersatz parlourmaid, but I compromised by agreeing to exchange my navy blue overall for a white one if she bought it. She did – but I was never allowed to take it home with me, it was kept at the flat, and when it was dirty I washed it there. A trusting soul was Mrs R-S.

Most of the visitors at the At Homes were of her generation – and her kind, decayed gentry. They held an awful fascination for me. It was as though I was turning back the clock some forty years to glimpse into the past. It was like a live photograph album. There were these people who had lived through an age of social and domestic revolution, who had endured two world wars, had seen the dissolution of the British Empire and with it the demolition of everything they stood for and believed in; yet had seemingly been untouched by it all. It was as though they had faced a siege and, as their numbers had been reduced, had withdrawn further inwards but had refused to surrender.

They would not come to terms. So long as there were those like themselves who they could be with, they were able to ignore the changed and changing world. And in their own or Mrs R-S's drawing-room, to the sound of tinkling teacups and soft voices talking of holidays in Bath or Harrogate with Lord and Lady This, referring to our dear Queen, and discussing the deficiencies, not of their servants but of their 'dailies', they felt safely protected from the violence and unkindness of the outside world – a world they had dropped out of.

One of the greatest shocks I gave Mrs R-S was on the day that Mrs Rutherford-Wallace came to lunch. Mrs Rutherford-Wallace belonged to the most élite of the Rutherfords – Mrs R-S spoke of her as though she was the Czar of All the Russias. She was a sort of doyenne of all the Rutherfords. When she married a Mr Wallace, he it was who insisted on her name being added to his.

When I heard about this relation, and that she was very old, I felt like saying to Mrs R-S, Well, perhaps when she passes on you may be able to get some more money by adopting yet another name and becoming Mrs Rutherford-Wallace-Smith! But I saw no point in straining our relationship to breaking point.

On the day that Mrs Rutherford-Wallace was expected, I was asked to cook and serve the lunch. I agreed at the same rate of pay as I was getting for the charring. I must have been green! I suppose I accepted because I liked cooking, and when I could select the materials without considering the price, I enjoyed it even more.

I was treated beforehand to a lecture on Mrs Rutherford-Wallace by Mrs R-S. She warned me not to take umbrage at her abrupt manner. 'She's very autocratic in her attitude towards servants,' she said, as if she herself was all sweetness and light. I wondered what I'd let myself in for.

Anyway, the day arrived and so did the great lady – very much the *grande dame* she was too. Although I say it, I cooked an excellent lunch and everything went off fine. I even got the serving right. I was always petrified with fright at doing it. I had recollections of the first time I'd waited at table, when I'd shot the potatoes down a visitor's cleavage, and the impolite language that had ensued.

Everything went smoothly until I took the coffee into the drawing-room. Mrs Rutherford-Wallace was talking about a nursing home that she'd been in under observation for a suspected duodenal ulcer, and she was saying, 'They want me to have an operation, but I don't think it's necessary.' I completely forgot my place. 'Not on your life,' I said. 'Don't let them use the knife on you, it's quite unnecessary. I was in hospital six weeks with an ulcer. They didn't operate on me and I'm as fit as a fiddle now.' Then I looked at Mrs R-S's face – she was horrorstruck. I waited for the storm to break from Mrs Rutherford-Wallace. Instead of the storm I got the sun – her face beamed at me, then she said, 'Sit down, gel, and get yourself a cup of coffee! Tell me all about it, what treatment you had and what diet you were on.' And before you could say knife, there we were, talking like two buddies. Mrs R-S couldn't get a word in edgeways. Eventually I managed to break away to do the washing-up but the *grande dame* later came out to the kitchen with some query, and as she left she slipped a pound note in my not unwilling hand. My stock rose with Mrs R-S, but not for long.

One morning when she was out, a man came to read the meter. I suppose he must have left the front door open, and, unbeknown to me, Henry waddled out into the great wide world. When Mrs Rutherford-Smith came back and found him missing I thought the heavens would fall on me! Never had such a heinous crime been committed. She nearly fainted in her emotion. I had to get the brandy for her. I also dosed myself liberally, too. I could see I was going to need it.

The porters from the block her flat was in were despatched to go round all the nearby houses to see if somebody had taken him in. 'That's a joke,' one of them said to me, 'who'd take in a mangy bleedin' Peke like 'Enery?' What a way to talk about a descendant of the Royal House of China. Talk about *lese majesty*!

The police were called in and I had to trudge for miles in the broiling sun – well, it seemed broiling to me. What I said about Henry is unprintable. I got back after a couple of hours and still he hadn't been found. Mrs Rutherford-Smith was prostrate with grief. Then I heard a sort of snuffling outside the front door. I opened it and there on the mat was an extremely bedraggled, but otherwise unharmed, Henry. While I was glad to see him, I did give him a quick one up the backside for the trouble he'd caused. Just then Mrs R-S came to see what was happening. She didn't say anything to me at the time, she was too busy lavishing kisses on her errant dog. But from then on her attitude towards me changed. Her demeanour was grave whenever she looked at me, so I wasn't surprised when, on the Friday, as she handed me my pay packet, she said, 'I've enclosed an extra week's money in lieu of notice – not that I blame you over Henry's escapade, but it has become evident to me that you feel no affection towards him and since, to me, he is an integral part of my household, your presence here is no longer welcome.'

Well, that was it. I'd lost my job because of a dog. How were the mighty fallen. Mind you, even if she hadn't seen me kick Henry up the bum, I think she'd have still got rid of me for I'd been a constant reminder of the day she lost her darling.

11

It was summer when I got the sack from Mrs R-S. The good thing about looking for a job in the summer in a seaside town is it's always easy to get one, especially daily work, because many women who are 'dailies' in the winter work in hotels and restaurants as soon as the town gets its summer visitors. They prefer an impersonal employer to one who's always taking an interest, because taking an interest can often mean criticizing and interfering. And although hotel work isn't as well paid, or it wasn't then, there's always the tips, which bring the money up to more than you get by going out charring.

I did try doing hotel work once or twice because my sister was doing it and we thought it would be more congenial working together. She's an excellent waitress although she was never in domestic service: she started working in factories when she left school. She does silver service now, which requires a high degree of skill. On the one or two occasions that I tried waiting, not only was I incapable of carrying more than two plates at a time, but since I was always thinking of the fiasco with the potatoes I became a nervous wreck. I was terrified, particularly when I was carrying dishes on a salver.

So I very soon got a charring job, and stayed there for over two years. It was with a nice couple who lived a quiet and uneventful life, and so did I working for them. They liked me, they appreciated my work, and I appreciated working for them, and if they hadn't left the town I probably would have worked even longer there.

When they left I was given a marvellous reference. Not that you really need a reference now. If you were asked for one you could always say, 'Oh, I haven't done daily work for years,' but often employers were so pleased to get help that they didn't ask for them. There were exceptions. Some people who were wealthy and had valuable things around naturally wanted to know about you, but generally they were prepared to pay more for that privilege. I've always thought that we, the workers, ought to be able to ask our employers for a reference too!

By now factories were taking on part-time women workers so as I'm prepared to try anything once, I went along and got a job. It was making parts for something or other – I forget what it was now. I was on shift work for four hours a day. One week it was four hours in the morning, the next week four hours in the afternoon. Somehow, I couldn't take to it at all. I seemed to have no kind of meaning there. I was just a cog in a machine and it was impossible to take a pride in the work. At least when you're in a house and you've done a room out, you see the results – gleaming floors, polished furniture, sparkling glass and so on, and you can stand back and look at it and say, There's a job well done. But how can you think that in a factory? All I did was to fit bits together, then put what they made on a slow conveyor belt. At the end of the four hours I'd just wasted time in exchange for money. I'd got nothing out of it except cash. It was lively enough, all women together; the language was terrible, and the conversation a sort of hotch-potch of sexual and social clichés against a background of blaring radio music.

While I was doing this mundane factory work I thought I needed some sort of lively activity, so I started attending evening classes for drama and mime. I had visions of myself as a great dramatic actress – mind you, I've had visions of myself as everything under the sun during the course of my life. They've most of them never materialized but I've had fun while the visions lasted. I started this class with a friend of my own age, but she speedily gave up.

One of the first things we had to do was to lie on the floor and relax. It's a wonderful word, relax – it's a respectable way of doing nothing, like Albert of an afternoon. He sits in a chair and goes off to sleep and afterwards he says he's been relaxing. It makes me laugh. I say, 'What you really mean is you're a lazy old lump loafing around idling your life away, but you call it relaxing because it's a nice word to salve your conscience with!'

Anyway, in this drama class we had to lie on the floor and relax. Not only was the floor far from clean, which worried

126

both my friend and me, but though it was fairly easy to lie down, my friend had the utmost difficulty in getting up and her efforts to do so were very funny but not respectable. So she packed it in. But, as usual, I stuck it out to the bitter end.

And believe me, it was bitter, because on the drama side I was never allowed to say more than 'Rhubarb rhubarb' in the crowd scenes, and my miming was hopeless. Why I should have thought I would be any good at it I don't know. I suppose I've always been an incurable optimist. When I started, I thought of that famous French mime, Marcel Marceau. Then I thought of French cooking and how I'd been able to master that, so I could see myself on top of the ladder before I'd got my foot on the first rung.

At the end of the term we had to take a test. What happened was we each drew from a hat a slip of paper on which was written the scene we had to mime. We weren't allowed to show it to the other members of the class, who had to guess what we'd portrayed or represented. I don't believe even Marcel Marceau could have done anything with mine.

I had to call on my grandmother who was ill. I was taking her a bunch of flowers and half a dozen eggs; my grandfather was so fed up with people who kept coming to the door that he wouldn't open it. Well, could you see me as Little Red Riding Hood to start with? I looked more like the Pantomime Dame! There I was with an imaginary bunch of flowers under my arm and in one hand a bag which was supposed to contain half a dozen imaginary eggs. How anyone could see they were eggs without my dropping them and trying to make an imaginary omelet, I don't know. I walked up to the imaginary door and I knocked my hand through it, and nobody came. So I knocked again, tapped my feet impatiently, then stepped back from an imaginary porch and looked up at a pretend window where I knew my grandmother was. That got me nowhere. Then I tapped my feet again, and if you've got feet my size you don't want to draw attention to them. Then I went back to the door, or the place where the door ought to have been, and I banged very hard with both fists, forgetting of course that to have done this I must have dropped the eggs, so they did get broken after all. I didn't bother to pick them up, they'd have made my hands sticky. I made out that the flowers were still under my arm so I put on a show of leaving them on the doorstep, pulled a face, walked away, looked up at the pretend window, and then went off.

Well, when the class were asked what I did, seventy-five per cent hadn't a clue at all. One said I was the milkman calling for the money, and another said I was trying to break into the house. Then one woman who I'd never fancied very much anyway said I'd come back home from work early because I suspected my husband was having an affair with another woman. I'd tried to get in and when I couldn't I'd left some things on the step so that the woman would fall over them when she came out. Then I'd gone away to wait for her with murder written all over my face.

Well, there's a charming classmate to have had for a term. Can you wonder I was disappointed? But how *could* I have mimed it? I just don't think it was on. Mind you, some of the students were so good you could tell at a glance what they were doing. I came to the conclusion it wasn't only the actions, it was the facial expressions that told so much and, according to my classmates, all I could do was look evil. So my theatrical dreams were shattered.

But it was ludicrous me visiting my grandmother anyway, because Albert and I had just become grandparents ourselves. I found this a very sobering thought, because our generation had always associated grandads and grandmothers with people of great age. I well remember both my grandmothers – they always dressed in black, had white hair and faces so lined they reminded me of a contour map.

One of them always wore a lace cap indoors – Queen Victoria used to wear one apparently – and she was a great admirer of Queen Victoria. She also used to wear a velvet bonnet when she went out. So that when Albert and I had now joined the ranks of these venerable persons, I wondered whether we shouldn't kit ourselves out to fit the part. We soon found, though, that young people today don't regard their grandparents in the way we did. I used to revere mine when I was young, revere them and fear them, in a way. They'd lived so long that they must know what could or could not be done,

128

and they jolly soon told you and no argument. But today young people know they're the only ones who possess the knowledge, so there's no point in looking venerable if you're not getting any credit for it.

By this time, of course, feeling as I did about it, I'd given up the factory job and it was this business of being a grandmother that made me look for another because as I said one day to Albert, 'We've got a christening present to buy and it's got to be something silver, too, not any old thing.' I could see by the expression on his face that our present state of finance didn't run to silver. It was in fact Albert who got me my next job.

He was unloading furniture in Brighton and started chatting to a woman next door who asked him if he knew of anyone who wanted morning work – Tuesdays and Saturdays. Albert said he thought his wife might be wanting a job. He didn't commit himself. He mentioned it to me and, although I really wanted three mornings, this was a start, so I went after it.

It was cleaning for two spinster women, a Miss Brockway and a Miss Field. Miss Brockway was a tall, hefty looking female – she made two of Miss Field.

At that time I had no idea that they were living together for mutual comfort and love. In those days one didn't always assume, as people seem to now, that two of the same sex in one place means a deviation from the norm. I merely thought that they shared a place for reasons of economy and companionship. In any case, I knew next to nothing about female sexual relationships. The only experience I'd ever had was when I worked as a cook in domestic service for a Mr and Mrs Bishop. A new parlourmaid joined us who got very friendly towards me. She often bought me sweets and such-like, and if we walked together, she'd put her arm round me.

I didn't really like these demonstrations of affection but, not wanting to hurt her feelings, I didn't protest. Then one night I was woken by her trying to climb into bed with me. I was horrified! When she saw how I felt she made up some tale about having had a dreadful nightmare and she had come to me because she was frightened. I suppose I believed her, but I locked my bedroom door after that! I may be doing her an injustice, she may not have had any other motive, but I have a suspicious nature. Also, she got on very well with Mr Bishop, and as he had the peculiar aberration of fingering the maid's hair curlers, they may have had something in common.

Miss Field was small and dainty-looking; she didn't go out to work, but stayed at home all day, so there was always someone to chat to. One of the first things I noticed was the beds. Although they didn't share a bedroom, the bed in Miss Field's room had a big dip in the middle and, since Miss Field wasn't very heavy, it struck me as strange. Looking back, I must have been very naïve because I remarked on this to Miss Field. She said, 'Oh, please don't let Miss Brockway hear you say that!'

It wasn't until I'd been there several weeks and seen the two of them around on Saturday mornings that I realized that they were living together in more senses than one.

I don't know how, but they seemed to know that I'd cottoned on, and I think that they were both relieved when they knew that I understood but wouldn't be leaving the job. I saw no point in leaving. It was well paid, I was getting five shillings an hour from them, and the way they behaved was their concern, not mine.

Miss Brockway, who was by far the more intelligent, then began to talk to me quite openly about their way of life. I felt embarrassed at first, because it wasn't exactly in my usual conversational orbit, but I got used to it. It's so much discussed nowadays that one would think there was some special merit attached to being a lesbian or homosexual; as though *they* were the norm and heterosexuals slightly peculiar.

My employers couldn't be identified by their clothes. Miss Field's were undistinguished but feminine. Perhaps Miss Brockway dressed a little mannishly – I don't think she consciously did, I think she just liked tailor-mades. It couldn't be said that either of them looked the part.

At that time there was no literature on the subject, or if there was, none of it came my way. I hadn't heard of *The Well of Loneliness*. And if I had, I'd have no idea of what it was about – I'd have thought it was a P. C. Wren novel about an oasis in the desert!

In these so-called enlightened times there are the intellectuals quoting Sappho and Plato and excusing it because it was a historical practice. I suppose if you feel that any way of life needs excusing it's possible to find historical justification for it. Though why you should have to bother, I don't know – it's surely better and easier just to accept it.

Mind you, neither Miss Brockway nor Miss Field bore any resemblance, physically or mentally, to Sappho and her lyric poetry, and certainly the band of lovely maidens that were with Sappho on the Island of Lesbos must have been very different from the motley collection that congregated where I worked on Saturday mornings. They may have been maidens, but when you've said that you've said the lot!

On Tuesday mornings Miss Field, or Sylvia as she asked me to call her, would talk about life as she and people like her lived it. She'd said to me, 'I expect you think I've missed a lot in life by not having normal sex but I saw too much of it as a child. My parents were very poor and I had to sleep in the same room with them, and, although I suppose they tried to be careful, I was conscious at an early age of what went on and it revolted me. My father drank and he was always giving my mother babies. She had ten children. My mother hated my father and so did I, and that's why I can't bear men to touch me, although I like them to talk to.' So I said, 'Well, your mother couldn't have hated your father all that much to have had that many children.' 'Oh, he forced himself on her,' she said, 'and once she'd got some she had to stay with my father so that he'd keep them.' It's just as I've said, you can find justification for anything. Criminals of any class blame it on their upbringing, and today everyone blames the television for the violence of our times. It's excuses, excuses. If some of the images I've created in my mind from reading books were put on the screen, even Kenneth Tynan would blow his top.

From the way she went on about it, I sensed that Sylvia, despite what she said, felt she'd missed out on life. So I'd console her by saying, 'I don't know. Like many things in life that are there for the asking, sex isn't all that exciting. When you first discover it, it's like caviare and oysters, but it ends up by being good old fish and chips!'

Needless to say, Albert didn't like me working there, but as he'd got me the job, he wasn't really in a position to raise any objections. Occasionally I'd have guilt feelings; I felt a bit of a Peeping Tom, or voyeur as they call it now, then I thought, Don't worry girl, put it down to experience. I was seeing a bit of life, something quite out of the ordinary. It wasn't likely to affect me, I'd got a husband and children and this lesbian lark couldn't have rubbed off on me. I believe some married women do have inclinations that way, and of course men who like other men get married, much to the grief of both husband and wife, generally. But I knew as far as I was concerned it wasn't anything contagious.

Sylvia in another mood would almost rhapsodize over her relationship with Miss Brockway, or Bertha. It would be a sort of beatification of Bertha. I found it difficult to keep in the right context; I used to find myself substituting the name Bill for Bertha; that way it made sense to me. She'd tell me that she was the great love of Bertha's life, that Bertha had tended to her every need for two years and protected her from other demanding females, and that God had blessed their union. But since, as far as I could see, very few heterosexual marriages were made in heaven, it seemed most unlikely that her kind of marriage would have been.

Although I suppose lesbianism isn't a subject for mirth (though I think if more people laughed about sex instead of putting it on the high altar, the world would be a happier place), I couldn't help laughing some Saturday mornings when they had their gatherings at the way they talked, particularly the remarks they made about men; they sent the sex up something shocking. Even their opposites in deviation, the male homosexuals – and one would have thought that they'd have had some sympathy towards them – were mimicked and satirized.

Bertha would have it that all the great feats of women had been done by people of their persuasion. She said that only women who had no place for men in their lives could have been single-minded enough to achieve them. 'Look at the suffragettes,' she said, and when I pointed out to her that the most famous of them all, Mrs Pankhurst, was a happily married woman, and many others had husbands who actively helped them, she said, 'I bet they made very unsatisfactory wives!'

It's my opinion that it was the newspapers who did their utmost to sort of unsex the suffragettes, just as today they try and make freaks out of students who protest or anyone who goes against the Establishment. And of course the men were prepared to believe what they read. They wanted women to be kept down. Equal rights, they felt, was a denigration of their manhood.

Although, as I've said, in appearance those that came to the house seemed normal and, unlike men, had no fear of being prosecuted, they seemed at times a very lonely and miserable collection. But when alcohol had flowed freely they could be really hilarious, revelling in their deviation as if they had received first prize in the lottery of life. At times, Sylvia told me, she and Bertha had terrible rows. Every day when Bertha came home from work there was always an inquisition as to what Sylvia had been doing. On some Tuesday mornings I would find Sylvia in tears, and it appeared that the intensity of their quarrels was greater than between a husband and wife.

Sylvia often went to a pub at lunchtime to have a meal, because she at any rate liked men's company, though she insisted to me that she only liked them to talk to, that she found them more intelligent than women. But I had my doubts when I found from time to time she received a present from some man. I found it very hard to believe that she got presents for conversing.

One day she showed me some fur gloves she'd had as a present. She made up some story about the man being a traveller and that these were a specimen sample. This seemed thin to me. It must have to Bertha. Apparently she had been so incensed when Sylvia spun her the yarn that she'd cut them up with a pair of scissors and thrown the pieces in her face.

Occasionally Bertha gave me one of her suits or dresses – we were much of a size. When she did, Sylvia would sulk around as though Bertha had discarded her, not the dress.

One thing I couldn't do was to try anything on in front of Bertha. I was probably very stupid about this. When she suggested it I went all coy. It wasn't that I expected her to make a play for me. I suppose it was that I'd got so used to thinking of her as Bill not Bertha that it would have been like changing in front of a man.

One occasion of very high drama was when Bertha's sister, Mrs McCullough, came to stay. She'd lost her husband some six months before, but as he'd been ill for a long time and had become just a vegetable, she wasn't by any means a forlorn widow. After a few days it was noticeable that Mrs McCullough had developed an affection for Sylvia. Not that she was tarred with the same brush as her sister. I think she just wanted friendship, someone, perhaps, she could be a mother to. She'd had a family who'd all grown up, and Sylvia was small, appealing and pretty, and, perhaps because she was the passive partner, a bit child-like.

Mind you, her appearance lied, because actually she was as tough as old boots. I think it was when Sylvia discovered that Bertha's sister had been left a lot of money that she began her plan of campaign. This was to go to Scotland with Mrs McCullough as her companion. To that end she applied all her feminine wiles; she played the sweet unprotected child, hung on Mrs McCullough's every word and gazed at her with wide adoring eyes – talk about Little Nell! She sang the praises of Scotland, with its glens and lochs. If she'd bought a set of bagpipes and started playing them I wouldn't have been surprised.

It was on a Saturday morning that Mrs McCullough said she must go home on Monday, and that she would like to take Sylvia with her – just for a visit, she hastily explained, after seeing the look on Bertha's face. While the scene that followed was ludicrous to an outsider, it was tragic to the protagonists. Bertha went through all the emotions, from self-sacrifice to dignified acceptance, buckets of tears to floods of invective. Through it all Sylvia, despite her declared passion for Bertha, was completely disinterested, but Mrs McCullough was also in tears and she decided to leave there and then, and without Sylvia. Sylvia went white with fury.

She got her own back, as I knew she would. For about three weeks she sulked around the place – not saying a word to a soul. She'd disappear the moment the pubs opened and, according to Bertha, who used to pour her heart out to me, came back drunk every evening. One Saturday morning she'd gone out at opening time as usual, then came back about an hour later with, horror of horrors, a man with her! 'Meet Harold Taylor,' she said. 'Harold and I are getting married.'

I looked at Bertha, and quickly looked away again. She'd taken too much. She let out an oath, then she went berserk. She threw china and saucepans, anything she could lay hands on, at Sylvia and her man Harold. Then she went at him with a broom. I thought, Any minute murder will be done. But Harold was no sacrificial lamb, he got out as fast as he could and left Sylvia to her fate! Then it was Sylvia's turn. She opened the window and screamed at his retreating figure: 'Bastard! Coward! Just like all bloody men – no guts!' Personally, I didn't blame him – one woman scorned is bad enough, but two!

Directly Sylvia turned her wrath on Harold, Bertha's attitude changed. She knew she'd won her battle, not only her battle of the sexes but her battle with her sister as well. Exhausted with exercise as well as emotion, they fell into each other's arms. I, needless to say, made myself scarce.

This was the beginning of the end for me. Although they'd had the grand reunion, they continued to quarrel about the circumstances that had caused the upsets, and individually they would ask me to arbitrate – 'Don't you think this, Margaret?' or 'Don't you think that?' Well, I knew enough about life to realize whatever I said was bound to get me into trouble with one or the other of them, and that finally they'd both gang up on me. So I called it a day. Mother broke her leg again and I was looking for a job.

12

AFTER my experiences with Bertha and Sylvia, Albert was determined that he would have no hand in getting me another job.

Jobs that were any good weren't easy to find in 1960. There was a lot of unemployment among men and women in both Brighton and Hove, and it was winter when work is always harder to come by there.

Yet, in spite of this unemployment, the record of drunkenness in Hove was the worst for twenty-four years. But perhaps that isn't so strange, because when men lose their jobs, are out of work week after week and can see no prospect of finding a job, they get so depressed and despondent that they spend their dole on drink to forget their troubles.

I know something about this at first hand, because after we had been married only six months Albert lost his job, and it was another six months before he got work again, and although in those days the dole was barely enough to keep us alive, we just had to have the occasional drink to keep us going.

Another difficulty was to find a place where there wasn't a dog. After my experience with Henry, I felt that it would be better for all concerned that way. But it seemed that only dog lovers wanted a 'daily'. As I went round answering advertisements, I'd ring the doorbell and up would start a loud yapping or woofing, then my heart would sink. The door would open and a dog would hurl itself at me. Then, on cue, the owner would always say, 'It's all right, he won't hurt you – he's only being friendly,' but I thought it was carrying friendship too far.

Nevertheless, the dogs won in the end. I was getting nowhere and eventually had to settle for one day a week with Mrs Marshall and her poodle. These dogs were very fashionable at this time: according to experts, Brighton and Hove were the most poodle-conscious towns in Britain. I burst my seams with pride when I heard that!

Mrs Marshall was a widow. Like so many of her kind she

had come down to live in Brighton after her husband had died. A lot of people fall into this trap of lifting their roots late in life. They take a bungalow or a flat by the sea and find, on a lower income, with time on their hands and no friends to spend it with, that they're bored and lonely. Only a short time ago the Medical Officer of Health for Brighton drew attention to this, and from my experience I know that he's right. Loneliness and fear are akin, and unpleasant companions to spend the last years of your life with.

I got to know little about Mrs Marshall. She was a pleasant person to work for, but she was very reticent – not a snob, but she never spoke of her earlier life. Once I did mention her husband, but she quickly changed the course of the conversation; perhaps she was fond of him, perhaps she hated him. Either way she didn't want to talk about him, so that was all right with me.

Mrs Marshall's poodle and I decided on a policy of mutual contempt. When I went into a room he left, and if he was in his basket, even if I wanted to move it, I left it alone. That way we managed to put up with each other.

Although Mrs Marshall didn't speak about her own life, she was kind and considerate about other people's. I've always tried to leave my troubles at home when I've gone out to work and I suppose that one of my virtues was that I was generally always bright and cheerful, though occasionally my laugh has caused some consternation.

If ever I was off colour or depressed most of the people I worked for thought I was sulking. 'Margaret's got out on the wrong side of the bed,' they'd say. Not Mrs Marshall, she'd sense that something was wrong and would be understanding and sympathetic. Yet she had enough to put up with on her own account; crippled with arthritis and often in great pain, she never complained. She could have done with me there every morning, not just once a week, but she couldn't afford it. One thing I was glad I was able to do was to help her with her shopping each morning. She didn't live very far from me so I'd collect her shopping list each day and drop the things in on my way back home; it helped her and didn't really cause me much extra exertion.

Another thing that shows how very fond I was of her is that one day, in a very rash moment, I let Mrs Marshall persuade me to go with her to a Dog Show. Never again, that I can say for sure! I've never seen such a carry-on in all my life. There were the owners, brushing, polishing and grooming their animals as if their lives depended on it. The pandemonium was indescribable. There were big dogs with deep baying voices, others that just barked, and yap yap yapping from the multitude of lap-dogs. There was a fight between two bull terriers and later a fight between two owners to decide whose fault it was.

But the thing that really sent me was a dog there wearing *navy blue pyjamas*! And it was the last sort of dog you'd have expected to wear any clothes, let alone navy blue pyjamas – an Old English Sheepdog! Rule Britannia! While I was exploding in laughter, some doggy person said it wore them because it was a wet and dirty day. That's as maybe, but every time I see an Old English Sheepdog, I think of navy blue pyjamas.

Mrs Marshall had another pet, a parrot, a grey one. It was a good talker – I believe the grey ones are better talkers than the pretty green and yellow ones. To compensate for the fact that they're nothing to look at, you get a lot of chat out of them. When I mentioned this parrot to my family, some of them made an odious personal comparison!

Parrots live long, too. Mrs Marshall said hers had been in the family for years. It was in and out of its cage all through the day. Normally I can't bear to be in a room where birds are fluttering around out of their cages – it gives me the horrors. Even a couple of canaries flying round give me a creepy feeling. But this Polly I didn't mind a bit; he behaved in such a dignified manner. First he would fly to the mantelpiece and gaze into the large mirror, preening himself, then he'd fly over to the oak biscuit-barrel and sit on it, and that meant he wanted a piece of biscuit. Sometimes he'd perch on my shoulder while we had our elevenses and try to eat a piece of my cake. Although he'd a strong beak he never bit me.

His tiny beady eyes seemed to look right inside my mind. I hope he liked what he saw there. He must have done, he was very fond of me. Wise birds, parrots. I like them. I wouldn't mind having one myself.

Just one morning at Mrs Marshall's wasn't adding a lot to the family income so I was glad to get another two with a Mr Hardy. He'd just taken a new flat. Before that he'd lived for years in a residential hotel where my sister was working as a waitress. When he was moving he asked her if she knew anyone who would 'do' for him, so I got the job. And a very good one it was too – a new flat and new furniture made the work very easy.

This Mr Hardy used to make me laugh describing the elderly people in this hotel. According to him they hibernated there in the winter, when they got reduced terms. Between meals they'd sit in the lounge with every window closed, sunk in the armchairs looking like figures in a waxworks, so apathetic that you'd think that they *couldn't* move. Then the gong would go for a meal and they'd be up from their chairs and into the dining-room like ravenous hounds, as if there was a prize for the first in. Then they'd watch as the plates were brought in to make sure that nobody got a larger helping than they did. Talk about a zoo!

Although Mr Hardy was elderly and somewhat frail, he was a very pleasant person to work for. He didn't assume because I was a 'daily' that this was synonymous with a person of low intelligence. Often while he was reading *The Times* he would ask my opinion on some article, or we would discuss politics together – he, of course, was a staunch Conservative, while I was strictly non-party. I suspect all politicians. But that didn't prevent us from having amicable arguments as to how the country should be run.

Unlike most men, he was very fussy about how the work should be done, but I didn't mind that. In some ways I was interested in having an employer who was concerned in the way I did things. After all, it was his home and he was paying me.

Shortly after I started there, he was taken ill. He went into a private nursing home and it cost him – he showed me the bills afterwards – over a thousand pounds altogether. They charged for every single item, even for aspirins. I used to visit him every day and do any shopping that he wanted and, although it was very comfortable and he was well looked after, I couldn't see that it was worth that money. It made me thankful for the greatest social service in the world – our own National Health Service.

When he came out, Mr Hardy seemed to take on a new lease of life. He did much more and seemed to have a real interest in everything. Then suddenly he became ill and died almost immediately. Talk about a waste of money!

As it was summer, I wasn't out of work a fortnight before I got myself fixed up with another job, though I nearly didn't go there. The weekend before I was supposed to start, I ran into Mrs Pennifold, who'd been in the same ward with me when I was in hospital for cancer. She was having her bunions removed, and when I'd recovered from the shock of *knowing* I had cancer, we used to have a hilarious time together.

She had been a char all her working life, and her pungent comments about the people she'd worked for used to keep me in fits of laughter. It was the first time in forty years of marriage that she'd ever slept apart from her husband. And when I commiserated with her, she said, 'Don't be bloody daft, gal, it's bleedin' marvellous not to have that lump of belly and booze in the same bed with me!'

When I met this Mrs Pennifold we got talking and I told her that I was going to work for a Mrs Freeman. 'Not the Mrs Freeman of King Grove?' she said. 'You won't be there long unless Barney likes you. They've had no end of chars. Mrs Freeman is fine, but that Barney . . .!' Naturally, I thought she was alluding to Mr Freeman, so I said, 'Oh, it's amorous interludes with the husband, is it? Then it's out as far as I'm concerned.' 'No,' she said, 'it's not Mr Freeman – you don't see much of him – it's Barney, Mrs Freeman's father. He lives with them. He's about seventy, very spry, but a bit touched mentally, and unless he takes to you he'll drive you out of the place with his tricks.'

Well, I was in two minds about going there. It seemed a bit pointless since there were plenty of jobs going. Still, as I had promised, I decided to give it a trial.

The first week or two I was there I saw very little of Barney. Mrs Freeman took him out in the car, presumably to give me time to get used to the place. But after I'd been there longer she began to tell me about her father. They were a Jewish family, and while she and her husband weren't orthodox Jews, her father was, and he liked all the old customs kept up, which, she said, made things difficult at times. Though as I got to know Mr Randall, I thought that this difficulty was slight in comparison with some of his disconcerting ways.

Barney's father had escaped to England from one of the pogroms in Russia or Poland and had started up in Whitechapel as a tailor. When he died he left nine children and a great deal of money. But Barney Randall had speculated unwisely and lost everything, and here he was, poor, old and slightly batty, and Mrs Freeman was the only one of his six children that would put up with him and look after him. All the others wanted him sent into a home. And really it just shows what a kind couple they were to keep him there, because he was a terrible liability. One of his most unsociable misfortunes was that he suffered, and those around him suffered, from the wind after, and often during, meals. He couldn't control himself. When he started, Mrs Freeman would point to the lavatory; this unfortunately was at the end of a long corridor, so his journey there sounded like an artillery battery in retreat. Yet all Mrs Freeman would say was, 'Can you imagine how they'd react to poor old Father in a home?'

I said to her, 'Don't you find it rather embarrassing when strangers are around?' Mrs Freeman just laughed. She said, 'Well, yesterday morning when we were walking along he made a loud report and people were looking round, thinking a tyre had burst!'

They'd had to give up entertaining at home because of it. Apparently what made them decide to do this was when they had had the rabbi to dinner. He was talking about some friend he'd met. 'I saw him walking along Marine Parade and he stopped me and said—' and bang on cue Barney let one go. 'Well,' she said, 'I didn't know what to do or say; then fortunately my husband laughed and everybody followed suit. But it might have gone the other way in someone else's company.'

141

By the time I'd been working there a month or more, Barney decided he liked me – I think because I laughed a lot and was always ready to talk to him. Mrs Jones, the previous char, had stayed only two weeks – she called him a dirty old man. I must admit that he was a lecherous old boy. He would often creep up on me, especially if I was using the hoover and couldn't hear him coming, then he'd pinch me in the rear, or kiss me on the back of the neck. But after all, what harm could he do? At his age it could only be wishful thinking.

He got so he wouldn't let anyone put his boots on but me – a doubtful honour but someone had to do it for him because he'd no strength in his fingers. His sense of humour could be peculiar. One morning he was sitting in the garden in his carpet slippers, waiting for me to arrive to put his boots on. He liked to sit by the incinerator, and throw in the rubbish that Mrs Freeman piled up ready for him. This particular morning I was a bit late and he, I suppose, was irritated at having to wait for me, so he threw his boots into the incinerator with the rubbish. He wouldn't tell me where they were and by the time I had registered what he'd done with them, they were in a very sorry condition. He wasn't worried. 'That'll teach you to be late,' he chuckled.

From time to time, the other members of his family would come down to see their father, and it was pathetic to see how Barney would try to be on his best behaviour.

Although he was a bit senile, he could on occasions behave perfectly normally – apart from the cannon shots! He longed for one of his sons to take him back to London to live. He seemed to think a lot more of his sons than his daughters – I believe Jewish people generally do.

It was after one of his sons had been down, Sidney, who lived in Golders Green, that he disappeared. When I got to work that morning I went into the garden to see to his boots and he wasn't there. So Mrs Freeman and I searched everywhere. We went round the streets, called on the near neighbours, but he wasn't to be found. Then I discovered that, though he'd gone out in his carpet slippers, he'd taken his hat and coat. We waited until lunch time, hoping he'd wander back. Mrs Freeman was just about to phone the police when our telephone rang. It was a call from London, from Sidney. Mr Randall had turned up there. How he did it on his own we never found out. He wasn't supposed to have any money.

The following day Sidney brought him back and there was a terrible row. The only place for Barney was an asylum, 'preferably in a padded cell!' said Sidney. He went on about Barney having ruined his marriage, that they'd have to move from Golders Green, that they were disgraced in the eyes of their neighbours. A very excitable boy was Sidney.

What actually happened was that although Barney knew the name of the road where his son lived, he didn't know the number of the house. So he knocked on door after door, looking very pathetic with his white hair and his carpet slippers, asking for a Mr and Mrs Randall. He told the same story to all of them. How his son Sidney wanted to look after him and give him a home, but his daughter-in-law was a cold-hearted selfish woman who had put him in a place with a lot of other old people and how they were all being ill treated.

When he eventually found Sidney's house he was at work, but the daughter-in-law was there. He was taken by a neighbour, together with her opinion about hard-hearted relatives. Later there were phone calls from others, all in the same vein. Jewish people have very strong views on those who neglect their families.

Sidney, by this time, had been ordered to report back home by his wife and battle was joined. When it became obvious to him that his scheme had failed and that he would be sent back to Brighton, Barney the Pathetic became Barney the Outraged. He went into a long diatribe about the ingratitude of sons, including quotations from the Old Testament showing what would happen to those that dishonoured their father. But none of it moved Sidney with his wife in the room. Everlasting Hell was better than the Hell he would get from his wife if Barney moved in with them.

But the old man wasn't finished with them yet. If he couldn't get his way he could get his revenge, and he did. The next morning – here Sidney nearly choked with rage – just before he was to be brought back, a neighbour knocked on the door and told Sidney's wife that her father-in-law was passing water out of a bedroom window in full view of the ladies sunning themselves in their gardens!

Mrs Freeman by this time had had enough of her brother. 'What a pity you've got such low windowsills,' she said, and walked out of the room.

We kept a strict eye on Barney after that escapade. But what a fine person Mrs Freeman was, and her husband – both were so good to Barney.

One evening a week I used to, I suppose you'd call it 'father-sit' for them. I would play simple card games with Mr Randall, fending off his fumblings if he was in an amorous mood, and listen to his talk about his youth and exploits in the First World War.

I suppose because of his age, he had to make frequent trips to the lavatory, which meant me undoing and later doing up his braces. He couldn't reach them, and in any case his hands were so feeble that he couldn't have undone the buttons. One night he set off on one of these trips, then I heard him calling me. He couldn't get off the lavatory seat – he was stuck fast. 'Well, unlock the door and I'll pull you up,' I said. 'How the devil can I unlock the door when I can't reach?' he shouted. I went out into the garden and, climbing on a box, opened the lavatory window. It was a narrow one and I couldn't get through, but I could see, and it was hard not to laugh at poor old Barney wedged on the pan.

I got the bass broom through the window and tried to prod him up, but when the sharp bristles met his bare flesh he let out such a shriek that I nearly fell off the box! Then I got the garden hoe, wrapped it in a cloth and tried to shovel him out. I laughed then and I still laugh now to think of me perched precariously on a box trying to get poor Barney off the pan, him cussing at me for laughing and his legs, skinny as broom-sticks, waving frantically around. I then tried pulling the chain, thinking that the shock of cold water on his backside might budge him. The only effect was a further stream of abuse. Eventually I had to break the lock on the door to get him out. He didn't lock it again after that.

Although Mrs Freeman seldom complained, it must have been a great strain looking after Barney, and he was so spry

144

that it looked as if he was good for another ten years at least. Then, one morning, trying to be independent, he was moving his armchair from the fireplace to the window, and the effort was too much for him. He collapsed and died almost instantly. It was a great sadness for us in the house because, for all his awkwardnesses, Barney was a character.

After the funeral, which was attended by all his family, now weeping copiously when there was no danger of having to have him live with them, his will was read, and I was delighted to learn that, unbeknown to any of them, he had some money after all – ten thousand pounds, all of which he had left to Mrs Freeman.

You should have heard the howls of rage that went up from the rest of the family – a mother bereft of her young couldn't have been fiercer than his sons and daughters, who considered they had been deprived of their share. Talk about the Wailing Wall of Jerusalem! They were going to contest the will; Mrs Freeman had used undue influence on him – they threw all the law books at her. Mrs Freeman was unmoved. The will was dated a week after he had gone to stay with her. It was water-tight.

13

IT wasn't long after Barney died that my job with the Freemans ended. They decided that, as now they hadn't to look after the old man, they would like to go back to London to live. I was sorry to say good-bye to them, but my sorrow was lightened by the £25 that Mrs Freeman gave me before she left. She said that her father would have wanted me to have it – good old Barney, I thought. But it was also good of Mrs Freeman because, after all, whatever I'd done for her father, she'd paid me for.

She gave it to me in cash, too, which pleased me. At that time I had no bank account and I didn't feel that cheques were money: circumstances have since altered cases, I'm glad to say. When I showed the money to Albert, he suggested that I didn't spend it but stopped working for a few months and used it up gradually, whenever we got short. Albert was always far more careful and sensible with money than I was – not mean, far from it – but he would look ahead, whereas I'd spend it when I got it. In any case, he was a sort of barometer as far as I was concerned. He could tell when work was getting me down or was liable to affect my health, and he wanted to preserve me as long as possible – after all, he was getting on in years and his prospects of acquiring another treasure like me were getting more remote. There I was, a good housekeeper and cook, and a good pub companion – what more could he want? And I was probably easier to live with when I didn't go out to work, because sometimes I came home very irritable, sometimes downright bad-tempered, and since there was nobody to vent my ire on except Albert now, he got the lot. So his motives for wanting me to give up work weren't entirely noble and selfless.

Altogether, I had nearly six months off. It was what I call my Delusions of Grandeur Period, the time when I surrendered to my Walter Mittyish dreams of breaking away from my working-class environment – not in a physical sense, but intellectually and socially. I don't know why I had this strong desire to become Somebody; I wasn't pressured into it. In fact, Albert and my family were perfectly happy with me as I was. But there I was with this idea of being somebody. It was vanity, of course – all is vanity, as the preacher once said.

I didn't know how to set about it. I took stock of what talents I had – precious few they were. The main one was my ability to laugh and make others laugh, but I couldn't see that laughter was going to get me anywhere. I made a plan, and that was to go to as many meetings and lectures as I could. I went to dozens on every subject under the sun. I felt if I could become an intellectual I would at least be on the right road to becoming a Somebody. Talk about a camel walking through the eye of a needle! I'm sure one of the hardest things in the world is for a working-class person of middle age to become an intellectual. As you make the effort to acquire an education, avenues open up, each of which requires a lifetime's study. You can be – and I think that I am – sharp and cute, but that's only a veneer; to be a real intellectual you need to have the right kind of education and environment from childhood. I soon realized that there are areas of perception that I could never hope to enter, and means of expression that were and would remain a closed book to me.

However, I also discovered that my deficiencies were not a tragedy, that it wasn't arriving but the journeying that mattered, and that this was informative, interesting and often amusing. Take the Friendship Society I joined. I can't remember the exact name of this Society, but since the word Friendship figured in it and since I've always considered myself the friendly type, and since the accent was on learning through brotherly love regardless of class, colour or creed, I thought it was what I was looking for.

After I'd been there some half-dozen times and was thinking of becoming a fully-fledged member, some dozen of us brotherly lovers went into a café after a meeting, and while we were having cups of coffee and biscuits, one of the members who wasn't with us came under discussion. One of our group, who obviously had money and a good education, started criticizing this absent member and finally described her as 'common'. Well, that started it. I was up in arms at once. I knew that, when I wasn't there, I should be labelled as *common*.

In no time at all a violent argument followed and the party broke up in disorder. Some Friendly Society!

Well, not only did I not become a fully fledged member, I gave up going to the meetings. I've said that my education was just a veneer, well, in the same way their friendship was just a veneer.

Brighton and Hove were then, and still are great places for lectures, meetings and conferences; they go on winter and summer. Perhaps it's something about the air that stimulates people to talk. If so, it's done wonders for me. But the things that go on. The Labour, Liberal and Conservative Parties have all met there, every society and leading company have had conferences there, it's a sort of hot-bed of hot air. One week we had a meeting about Why Britain Should Join the Common Market, and the following week another devoted to

Why Britain Shouldn't Enter the Common Market.

Funnily enough, in spite of what I've said about the word, I don't mind the Common Market being called Common. I suppose it's because having listened to both meetings, I don't care what we do one way or the other. I'm bored with the subject. After all, I'm talking about 1962! We're not yet in the Market and they still go on about it today.

There was even, at that time, a meeting of publicans so that they could say that they didn't want to have to keep the pubs open until eleven o'clock at night, which they'd been told to do. There was a farcical thing. It didn't make much difference one way or another to Albert and me – there's always been enough time for us to spend what money we had in the pubs. Still, it's revealing, isn't it, that though publicans, like everyone else, expect social service as their due, they're not prepared to give the public service which surely is its right.

I was surprised at the interest now being shown in the new Sussex University. I thought the residents would be apathetic about it, but when the topping-out ceremony came in February 1962, everyone seemed very excited. They have these topping-out ceremonies when the roofs and the chimney pots are on the buildings; the architects, builders and whoever the buildings are for get together with the workers and drinks are taken.

As I say, great interest was shown. People went around talking about 'our' university. I must say they weren't quite so possessive about it a few years later when the student unrest started. They really went to town about them, tarring them all with the same brush. There's scant respect for learning in this country. I thought then that people knocked the students to excuse their own ignorance and stupidity, and I still think the same.

Somebody once thought up the phrase *Mens sana in corpore sano*, which saying was later responsible for the playing fields of Eton. I don't know how I picked it up. Anyway, alongside my going to classes and lectures I decided to join a keep-fit class.

It was for middle-aged women with ages ranging from about forty to sixty, so middle age covered a pretty wide radius, and the same could be said for our middle areas.

Some of us looked as though no amount of keep-fit exercises could ever do anything for us. It was obvious that we hadn't been fit for years – certainly not fit enough to parade around in swimsuits, as some of them did. And some even wore Bermuda shorts; has there ever been a more foul garment than that? Ill-fitting and flapping round the knees. Some wore slacks, but others, and this included me, were wary of displaying their ample rears and settled for a blouse and skirt.

We did a lot of our exercises to music, lying down on the floor and then getting up without putting our hands on it. We did press-ups, though some people, even when their arms were extended, still had most of their body on the floor. Then there was bending and stretching and touching the toes. Touching them – some people couldn't even see them! Anyone who thinks those bawdy postcards by Donald McGill far-fetched should have seen our class. It was great fun, though. We used to shriek with mirth – with us it was laugh and keep fat. But really it was a farce in every way because when you run a home you're doing far more keep-fit exercises going up and down stairs and bending and stretching making the beds.

Still, I threw myself into this class with the same enthusiasm that I gave to the others. I was determined to become lithe and lissom. When I told Albert this he wanted to know why. I don't think he was suspicious, just interested. I explained to him that the older you get the more you look back at the past and clutch on to the remnants of youth. My mother's now in her ninetieth year and I still have to wash and set her hair for her every fortnight, and she's terribly fussy about it.

When you're between fifty and sixty, you haven't quite said good-bye to your feminine charms. All right, you've got your husband, but it's still exciting if someone now and again casts a covetous eye on you. Not that you want to go to town with them (though chance would be a fine thing), it's that you want them to look as though they want to go to town with you. I don't know whether the other women in my class felt the same. Most of them were like me; in the interval we undid all the good that the exercises had done by scoffing tea and biscuits.

But what finished me were the Sunday afternoon rambles. Some bright person had the idea that a nice long hike on a

Sunday would peel the weight off. We could take our husbands if we liked, but Albert wasn't wearing this, not with a collection of mums, even if they'd been young ones. I explained to him that other husbands would be coming along. 'That's their business,' he said, 'if they want to make bloody fools of themselves, let them. I'm not.' Adamant he was. He was right, of course.

I know that, when I was a child, the Sunday afternoon walk into the country was a sort of time-honoured institution. We always used to do it in the summer and I enjoyed them, but then the country was nearer and walking wasn't the hazardous affair that it is today. First we'd have to catch a bus to reach the country, and once there we were all at sea, metaphorically speaking. We wanted to avoid the main roads, but everywhere there were notices up 'Trespassers will be prosecuted' or 'Beware of the Bull' – 'Beware of the Cow' would have been enough for me.

Then, when at last we managed to get off the road, it wasn't long before we came up against a mass of barbed wire that only an eel could have wriggled through. The fields were fenced in and the gates padlocked, so our rambles nearly always ended up with us walking along the grass verges of the roads, staggering along like drunken sailors, stopping occasionally to massage a ricked ankle or to replace a shoe that had got left behind in the mud. All the time sucking in the carbon monoxide from the cars that sped by. Talk about the shady nook and the rustic glade!

The only person who enjoyed these Sunday hikes was Albert. He thought they were lovely because he could go to bed and have a beautiful sleep! I used to come in dog-tired, covered in dust and as irritable as could be, particularly if he hadn't come down and made a cup of tea. When I found him asleep I'd be white with rage. No, for me the rambles were a shambles, and although I'd never really cared for the countryside, the opportunity of renewing my acquaintanceship with it didn't come. We never found it. So, along with the rambles, I packed in the keep-fit class. But it got me my next job.

Our instructress went twice a year to a nature establishment, where you pay fifty guineas a week to be pummelled, pinched and live on a starvation diet. It was in Hove, and I went there to work on her recommendation. She said that the owner was such a jolly, cheerful person – she didn't mention, of course, that the work was very hard.

I wasn't sorry to start again. By this time not only had my money run out, but while I wouldn't exactly say I missed work, I missed the kind of people I met when I was working. Again, while I hadn't got over the feeling of wanting to be somebody, I had got over trying to do anything active about it. Albert didn't mind me starting again. I think with the keep-fit classes and the hikes, he had come to the conclusion that I could get too strong in health. In any case, if anything went wrong with me in a nature cure place, it would be a matter of 'Physician, heal thyself'.

The owner's name, Mrs Welfare, was very appropriate to her establishment, though I later discovered it was her first husband's name, that she'd had two more since and had only recently divorced the third.

Why she was so unlucky in her husbands I never found out – perhaps it was because she was such an incessant talker. I reckon I can go on a bit, but Mrs Welfare could beat me hollow – hers was an ever-rolling stream. I wait for people to answer, but Mrs Welfare didn't, so perhaps her husbands felt left out of the conversation and that they would become dumb if they stayed with her any longer. She was quite philosophical about her marriages, trotting out the old saying 'There's as good fish in the sea as ever came out'. Still, at her age, I felt she would have to cast her net a bit wider for the next – after all, the older the fish are, the more wary they become!

The house was very old and very large, the type of house, in a way, that I'd worked in when I'd been kitchen maid and cook, because it had a huge basement and there were three floors above this. That was one of the reasons why the work was so hard.

She could accommodate six people, or eight if there were two married couples sharing. The other helpers were her sister, Miss Thompson, who was about forty, and who massaged some of the females, a young man, Norman, who did the same for either sex, and an odd-job man called Old Louie – and a cantankerous old thing he was.

Miss Thompson was righteousness personified. She looked as though she'd swallowed a sour apple and it had disagreed with her. She gave me to understand as soon as I got there that the reason she'd never married was because she had looked after her widowed mother until she died: 'It was my Christian duty to do so.'

Why we poor women should have to make an excuse about not being married I don't know. Today, of course, you don't, you what is called 'pad up' with a man if you want kids or take the pill if not. For her generation it was still considered something detrimental to womanhood not to be married, so you made up any excuse you could. I found her excuse hard to believe, as it's always the things that are your Christian duty to do which are the last things that you really want to do. It's like 'the will of God' – that's normally the stupidity of people. I hope I don't offend too many people when I say that Christ and His disciples seemed to have such a poor opinion of females on earth that many of us don't fancy finding a place in heaven.

Mrs Welfare's visitors, who usually stayed from two to four weeks, had great faith in her internal cleansing, weight reducing and vegetarian diet. I suppose if you're prepared to spend fifty guineas a week trying to regain health and beauty, you've got to start off with faith even if you don't end up with it. They say faith can move mountains, well, it needed to, in a literal sense, with some of Mrs Welfare's clients.

Take Mrs Joseph. She must have weighed at least fourteen stone. It was a splendid sight to go into her room in the morning and see her laying in bed with marrow-like breasts hanging over the sheet! I used to go away humming that tune 'Does Santa Claus sleep with his whiskers over or under the sheet?'

She caught me staring at them once, but she didn't mind. 'You might find it hard to believe,' she said, 'but there was a time when my husband called these objects his peaches, his Mounts of Venus!' Well, all I thought was, that must have been many years ago! There was a photograph of her husband

152

on the bedside table. He was a professor of something-or-other, with some obscure degree he'd picked up in America. He had a long beard and I could visualize them in bed together – her with the pendulous peaks and him with his beard hanging over the sheets. Let's hope she wasn't ticklish!

The treatment which Mrs Welfare's clients had to undergo when they arrived was drastic – I wouldn't have gone through it even if I'd been paid, let alone it costing a small fortune. For the first three days they had nothing but several doses of Epsom Salts and glasses of a grape wine that Mrs Welfare made. She got me drinking it – the grape wine, I mean, not the Epsom Salts, but it didn't do a thing for me.

After three days on these liquids, the patients were supposed to be cleansed of the impurities in their blood. But when I looked at them it seemed to me most of their blood had gone as well. When they were allowed to eat solids, they began on grated carrot, lettuce and other raw vegetables, still drinking the grape wine and being pummelled every day either by Miss Thompson or Norman.

Norman was about thirty-five. He was rather a good-looking man, and because of this he did well for tips from both the men and the women, especially the latter. If they could have known what he called them – parasites and lotus eaters were two of his milder expressions. I said to him, 'Why lotus eaters?' 'They lived in a land of perpetual nod, didn't they?' he said. 'They ate lotuses and this made them never want to go anywhere or do anything, they were happy just to waste their lives away. Mind you,' he added with glee, 'it didn't cost them fifty pounds a week, did it?'

There was a perpetual feud between him and Old Louie. They would vie with each other for the tips. Old Louie, despite being somewhat uncouth, and slightly batty, had one claim to fame. It appeared that some years ago, walking home through a dark road late at night, he saw a man attack a woman and, not being heroic enough to rescue her physically, he blew a police whistle, which he had but had no right to have. It saved the woman because the man ran away, and Old Louie was commended by the magistrates for his presence of mind, then fined for possessing a police whistle. Old Louie built this up into such a chivalrous affair that you'd have thought he was Sir Lancelot himself.

What would enrage me about that place was that the clients behaved like a bunch of children, only worse. There they were, paying fifty guineas a week to lose weight, yet they'd smuggle in bars of chocolate, or pay me to bring them bottles of Scotch or gin. I used to tell them that if they did my job and had to run up and down stairs umpteen times a day they could get paid for being there.

But of course, the sort of thing they were doing was much more pleasant than hard work. They'd gather in the morning in the exercise room and ride stationary bicycles or pull at a rowing machine. They felt the inches of excess flesh were melting away. Generally, the reason they wanted this to happen was so that their diet would get a bit more substantial, because they had to get a certain amount off before they were allowed to eat anything decent at all.

When I started there, my lunch caused a bit of trouble, because they were all vegetarians. On the first day I was served with some concoction called lentil cutlets. When I said that I wanted meat with my meal, you'd have thought I'd asked for rat poison! We eventually compromised; Mrs Welfare paid me more and I went without lunch.

Although it was hard work, it was never dull. There were visitors always coming and going. Miss Thompson added nothing to the gaiety of the scene but Mrs Welfare and Norman were generally cheerful and lively. I felt there was more than a working relationship between Mrs Welfare and Norman, despite the fact that she was so much older, and certainly Miss Thompson doted on him. It was only when he was with her that her face would twist into what passed for a smile and she used sweet words to him that were never visited on anyone else.

So I worked there for about two interesting but uneventful years. Then Mr and Mrs Pratt, an American couple who'd been touring England, arrived. Mr Pratt I disliked on sight; my first glimpse of him being in his underpants on his way to the bathroom. He was a hairy man. His chest and arms were so covered in hair that you could hardly see his skin. He oozed virility. They say hair is a sign of masculinity. I sometimes tease Albert by quoting it because he's only got five or six hairs dotted around on his chest.

When this Mr Pratt came back from the bathroom I was making the bed. I heard him sneak up on me and then he patted my posterior. I saw his bare feet behind me and pretended to step back in surprise, making sure my heel went hard down on his foot with all my weight on it. That did his virility a power of no good at all. He was hopping round the room for all of ten minutes. I can't stand bottom-patters; I think I prefer pinchers.

Such men as he are congenitally incapable of realizing that they are not God's gift to women, as I speedily told him when he tried to do the same thing again. Mind you, a lot of the men there were like him in that respect. I suppose when you eat like a rabbit you think you can behave like one.

Mrs Pratt was the antithesis of her husband, being overweight and at any rate giving no appearance of being sexy. Her dressing-table was covered with every pill under the sun, from simple aspirin and yeast tablets to hormones and testratin. She was a food faddist and she went in for psychoanalysis.

She talked about her analyst in America as though he was her pet poodle. She saw him twice a week and couldn't run her life without him. She was a great believer in Freud: she said that her problem came from being deprived of a mother's love. All this sort of stuff came out over a nut rissole, a couple of lettuce leaves and a glass of Mrs Welfare's grape wine.

How people can talk about themselves in this way to comparative strangers I don't know. You get it a lot. I'm now frightened even to glance at anybody on a train.

Mr Pratt seemed to be bored stiff with her. Mind you, he looked bored stiff when anybody except himself was talking, but as she was the one with the money, left her by her first husband, he had to put up with it.

I was wrong about Mrs Pratt. She may not have looked sexy but she got a thing about Norman. By the end of the second week she was tipping him lavishly for trivial services. She would ring her bell on any pretext to get him into the room. By the end of the third week she didn't have to ring, Norman was going in regularly on his own account. It must also have been on account of the money she was paying him, because as I've said, Mrs Pratt was no Sophia Loren. Mr Pratt must have known what was going on but he took no notice. I expect it was going down on the credit side against his own mis-demeanours.

Mrs Welfare didn't seem to worry either – still, she couldn't criticize, could she, having had three husbands herself? Miss Thompson, though, was furious. I would have thought that it was her Christian duty to put the best interpretation on Mrs Pratt's and Norman's behaviour, but oh no – it was immoral, filthy, almost incestuous. When her sister said that Norman's morals were none of her business, she went berserk. They had a terrible row. After Mr and Mrs Pratt left a week later I hoped that things would go back to normal. But two or three days afterwards this Miss Thompson and Norman had a terrible set-to.

Mrs Welfare sparked it off by saying to Norman that he was going to miss Mrs Pratt. Norman agreed, 'Yes, I am, she was a nice lady.' Then Miss Thompson exploded! '*Nice?*' she said, 'what do you mean, *nice*? She was a harlot!' That did it. Norman tore into her. He made mock of her spinsterhood, then gave her 'Christian duty' a good going-over. By the time he'd finished with her she was in screaming hysterics. I made myself scarce when it started but they could be heard all over the house.

The next day Norman wasn't there. He'd packed it in and so did I shortly afterwards, because it got so grim working there with Mrs Welfare wild at Miss Thompson because of losing Norman, and Miss Thompson even more sour with everybody because, through her jealousy, she'd exposed her feelings towards Norman.

But the strange thing was that the establishment didn't last long after that, because some few months later I was walking past the house and it was empty and up for sale. I reckon Mrs Pratt did for it. A pity she never knew. It would have given her and her psychiatrist a talking point for months.

Though my next job, three days a week charring in a block

of luxury flats, was uneventful, it was while I was there that my dream of becoming a Somebody began to transform into reality. I'd joined an afternoon discussion group. I didn't go there to learn, only to practise. The instructor was a Mrs Burnham, whose husband was the actor and producer Edward Burnham.

One day she asked me if I'd go the following week to a class she held at Haywards Heath. She said a Mr Crutchley who worked for the BBC was going to be there and that he was looking for ordinary people with an extraordinary ability to express themselves vocally. Well, I wasn't sure how to take this, but as I liked Mrs Burnham, I decided to go.

I didn't think this Mr Crutchley would turn up, but he did. He took over the class for a bit, and then asked two of us if we'd come and be recorded in another room – there was myself and a Scottish lady. She was interviewed first. He and I then seemed to spend hours chatting away into his tape recorder. When it was over he asked me if I'd like a drink. I tried not to sound too enthusiastic. I enjoy a drink any time, but after all that talking I was parched – so, by the way he swallowed his beer down, was Mr Crutchley.

Well, of course, we got chatting. He had one of those silky public-school voices which made what he said sound important and sincere, and he said some nice things about me. When we parted he said I'd be hearing from him, so I went back to Brighton highly elated. When I told Albert he wasn't so optimistic – 'You know what you've said about people who talk like he does. Never believe a word they say.' Well, I looked so crestfallen Albert took me out for a drink, to cheer me up. At least I wasn't doing too badly on the alcohol for one evening.

A couple of days later, by the same post, came three letters. One was from this Mr Crutchley – Leigh Crutchley, he signed himself. What a nice Christian name, I thought. Later I discovered that everyone called him Reggie – according to Jack de Manio everyone at the BBC's called Reggie whatever his real name is! Anyway, this Leigh, as I thought he was, said everyone was pleased with the recording, that I was to be one in a series of programmes called *It Takes All Sorts*, and that I should be getting a contract. The next letter I opened was the contract – so far so good.

The third letter had the heading 'Peter Davies, Publishers', and it was from a Derek Priestley, managing director, asking me to telephone and make an appointment to see him. Blimey, gal, I thought, when things happen to you they happen fast. It transpired that this Leigh or Reggie had spoken to Derek Priestley and told him he felt there was a book in me (which I thought was rather an impolite way to put it after such a short acquaintance!) and when I met Mr Priestley and chatted to him a bit, he said he thought so too and would I have a go. Would I have a go! I reckon I must have grown a foot during that week. Then I started writing and I knew what Churchill meant when he spoke about blood, tears and sweat. It took a long time, because not only was I writing, I was running a home, charring and studying for my 'O' and 'A' Levels in English. But regularly I was going up to the BBC and recording for Reggie Crutchley. He got me in feature programmes, on 'Woman's Hour', and several other programmes.

Although he had this charm that I mentioned earlier, he could switch it off in an instant. He did this to me regularly at first. One day, when I was near to dissolving into tears, I asked him why he was being so unkind. 'I don't want you to get spoiled,' he growled. 'Once you do, you're a dead duck.' Looking back, I know he was right. Even the small success I was having could easily have gone to my head. He never let it. He doesn't now, he's always deflating my ego.

Eventually the book, *Below Stairs*, was finished, accepted and published. What has followed was what I had always wanted, I was a Somebody. Not a big Somebody, but a person in my own right, a person people wanted to meet – and have I revelled in it! I've had a whale of a time. Oh – I stopped being a treasure a fortnight before the book came out.